THIS IS
BOTSWANA

THIS IS
BOTSWANA

Daryl & Sharna Balfour

Text by Peter Joyce

NH
NEW
HOLLAND

Photographers' dedication

For David, Cathy, Martin and Tiffany – our Maun family.

Photographers' acknowledgements

We would like to thank the numerous people and organizations who assisted us during our travels. We are especially grateful to:

The Government of Botswana – including the Office of the President and the Department of Wildlife and National Parks, for making it possible to explore the country and its splendid sanctuaries.

David and Cathy Kays of Riley's Garage, Maun, for opening their home to us and for all their many other courtesies, including the assistance they gave us with this project.

Alan Walkden-Davis of Shell Oil Botswana (Pty) Ltd for the essentials of travel – petrol and oil. Botswana is a vast country and we covered more than 15 000 kilometres in three months in our Isuzu 4X4!

The owners and management of the various camps, lodges and hotels, for their hospitality. Special among them were: Okavango Wilderness Safaris (Mombo and Jedibe); Gametrackers (Xaxaba, Khwai River Lodge and Santawani); Ker & Downey (Pom Pom, Shindi Island and Abu's Camp); Lloyd & June Wilmot of Lloyd's Camp, Savute; Randall J. Moore and Mike Lorentz for the elephant-back safari; Mashatu Game Lodge; Tuli Game Lodge; Chobe Chilwero; Photo Africa (Linyanti and Selinda); Chobe Game Lodge; Cresta Hotels and Lodges (Mowana Safari Lodge, Chobe, Thapama Lodge, Francistown and The President Hotel, Gaborone); and Jannie & Eileen Drotsky of Drotsky's Cabins.

Evelyn & Bing Weskob of Wildlife Helicopter Services, Maun, and to pilot Ray Sharples for his excellent flying, for help in obtaining the aerial photographs.

Tim Liversedge, the Okavango's Pel's fishing owl specialist, for co-operation in photographing these elusive birds.

Brian Schwartz and Trevor Pole both of Nikon agents Frank & Hirsch (Pty) Ltd in Johannesburg; Ezio Beretta and Fazel of Citylab, photolab, Sandton, Johannesburg; Delta Motor Corporation Ltd; Canvas & Tent (Pty) Ltd; Sean and Nina Beneke of SD General Spares, Mhlume, Swaziland; Bronwyn Myburgh in Maun for all the messages taken and passed; and Mich & Billy Cochrane, who always have a bed for us in Johannesburg and uncomplainingly run errands while we are isolated on assignment.

Last, but certainly not least, to Mom and Philip, who gave us a home from which to operate during our stay in Botswana, and much, much more.

Daryl and Sharna Balfour

First published in 1994 by New Holland Publishing
Garfield House, 86–88 Edgware Road,
W2 2EA London, United Kingdom,
www.newhollandpublishers.com

New Holland Publishing is a member of the
Johnnic Publishing Group

Second UK edition: 1999

10 9 8 7 6 5 4 3 2

Copyright © 1994, 1999 New Holland
   Publishers (Pty) Ltd
Copyright © 1994, 1999 in text: Peter Joyce
Copyright © 1994, 1999 in photographs:
Daryl and Sharna Balfour with the exception of:
A.A.N.S p. 19; MuseumAfrica pp. 22 (top), 23;
De Beers Photographic Library pp. 24, 31;
J. Lauré p. 21 (top); National Archives of Zimbabwe
p. 25; South African Library p. 21 (bottom).
Copyright © 1994, 1999 in maps:
   Loretta Chegwidden

ISBN 1 85974 269 6

opy editor: Sue Ryan
Editorial assistant: Christine Didcott
Text consultant: Alec Campbell,
   Botswana National Museum and Art Gallery
Designer: Darren MacGurk
Cover designer: Tracey Mackenzie

Reproduction by Hirt & Carter Cape (Pty) Ltd
Printed and bound Times Offset (M) Sdn Bhd

Log on to our photographic website
www.imagesofafrica.co.za for an African
experience.

FRONT COVER: *An aerial view of buffalo,
Okavango Delta*
SPINE PICTURE: *Red lechwe in Moremi
Game Reserve*

CONTENTS

Frontispiece: The painted reed frog, a common resident of the Okavango Delta.
Title page: Buffalo herd together on the Okavango's lush floodplain.
Right: A cheetah twosome in the Mombo area of the swamplands.

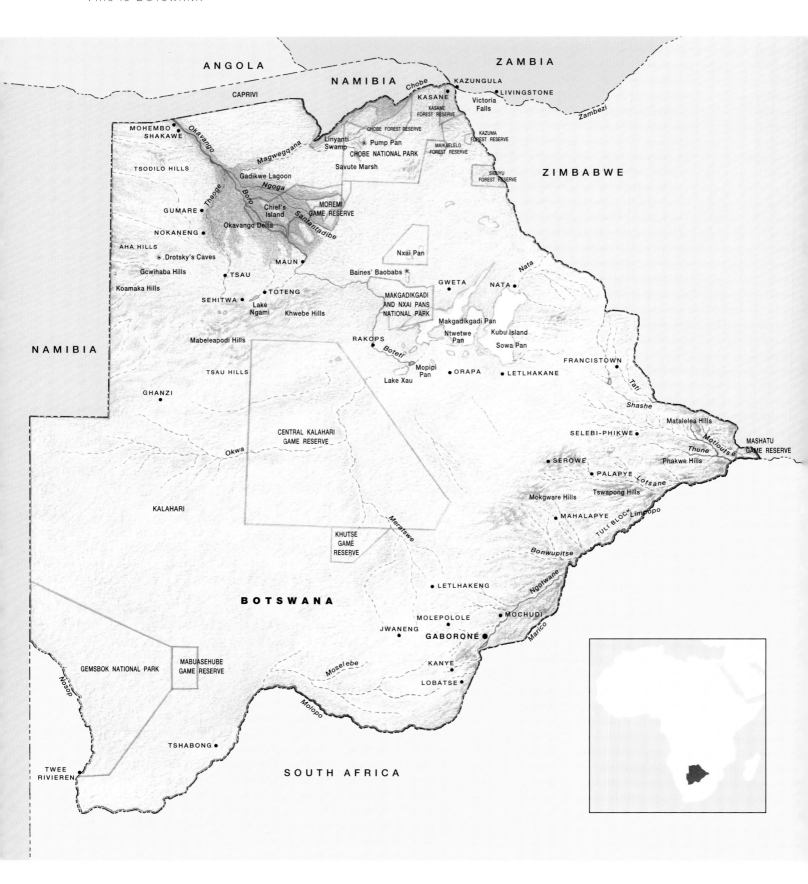

BOTSWANA PROFILE

Probably the most important word in Botswana, a word that holds profound significance for virtually every one of its inhabitants, is 'pula'. It means 'rain'. It is also a form of greeting, an expression of good wishes for the future, and the name for the national unit of currency, but these are secondary applications, definitions that simply emphasize the primacy of and pay tribute to the role of rain in this vast and mostly dry part of south-central Africa.

In Botswana, water is the most precious of all commodities. The great majority of the people depend in one way or another on the land for their well-being, and in many instances for their very survival, and the land, all too often, is unforgiving in its arid harshness. The rains are sporadic and unreliable; drought is the norm rather than the exception; huge tracts of territory have no surface moisture; the only permanent sources are the Okavango, the Linyanti-Chobe, and the tributaries of the Shashe and the Limpopo rivers, which bring sustenance to segments of the far northern region but leave the greater part of the country untouched.

These watercourses, however, and especially the first two, combine to make of Botswana one of the African continent's finest tourist destinations. The Okavango, born in the uplands of Angola to the north-west, flows into and then spreads over the sandy spaces of the Kalahari to form an immense and wondrous inland delta of lagoon and labyrinthine channel, palm-fringed island

and fertile floodplain. Scores of safari lodges and camps have been established in and around this watery wilderness, and in the game-rich Moremi and Chobe reserves farther to the north, and between them they offer visitors the best of several worlds, appealing variously to the game-viewer and bird-watcher, the hunter and the sporting fisherman, the explorer of hidden places and the lover of Africa at its loveliest and least spoilt.

Botswana, which in the old colonial days was known as Bechuanaland, is a big country, scantily populated, landlocked. Its modern name was assumed at independence in 1966 and is derived from the Setswana language, spoken by the largest of the ethnic groupings that in sparse and uneven fashion inhabit a region larger than France and only a little smaller than the American state of Texas. The population is at its densest in the comparatively well-watered south-east, along the common border with South Africa's Transvaal province. Botswana also shares frontiers with the Cape province in the south, with Zimbabwe in the east and north-east, and with the desert wastelands of Namibia in the west. To the north-west, in striking physical contrast, is Namibia's Caprivi Strip, a long, narrow and lushly vegetated finger of land distinguished by its rivers and marshlands. A tiny linear segment of this region, stretching just 700 metres from end to end, serves to divide Botswana from the Republic of Zambia – the world's shortest international boundary.

THE LAND

Botswana covers 581 730 square kilometres of the Great African Plateau, a gigantic geophysical feature that rises in the Sahara Desert 5 000 kilometres in the north to extend across most of the continent. In Botswana its elevation is at a fairly constant 1 000 metres above sea level, and for the most part the terrain is remarkably uniform, the flat, sun-baked monotony of the countryside unrelieved by hill, ridge or valley – a vast, empty land of blistering heat, sand and an infinite silence, of far horizons and, at times, a distinctive and haunting beauty. The main highways are new and in excellent condition, but for the independent traveller intent on exploring the wider spaces movement around the country can be difficult and, in the remoteness of the central and southern regions, even hazardous: distances are enormous, the roads rugged and little used, and if your vehicle breaks down help may be a long time in coming.

Bisecting Botswana from north to south is a broad strip of higher ground which, though scarcely discernible to the eye, nevertheless forms a dividing watershed. Running across to the east are seasonal streams that, when they do flow, give some sustenance to the ungenerous earth before joining the larger watercourses: the Marico, Shashe and Limpopo rivers. Once, long ago, liberal amounts of water from this modest tableland also drained westwards to help fill the great pans of the interior, and Sowa Pan still receives some seasonal replenishment from the Nata, Tutume, Mosetse and other such watercourses. Those from the north and northwest have also virtually dried up, and the great, shallow depressions remain dry for most of the time, their surrounds a desolation of Kalahari sandveld.

The Kalahari, which covers over two-thirds of the country, is commonly termed a desert because of its sandy soils and almost total lack of surface water, but most of the region is in fact vegetated, though sparsely so, and is more properly classed as a wilderness or 'thirstland'. The broad plains are mantled by a thin coat of grasses and savanna

The Central Kalahari Game Reserve is at the heart of the so-called Kalahari 'desert', which in reality is a region of rolling grasslands and scattered thornscrub interspersed with dense stands of drought-resistant trees.

thorn scrub, and in those areas where underground water lies close to the surface, the countryside resembles parkland. Botswana's only expanse of true desert is found in the extreme south, a region of high red dunes and ancient river-beds that extends into South Africa's Cape province.

Quite different in nature and appearance is the north-western segment of the country. This is still part of the Kalahari system, but it has been transformed by the Okavango, southern Africa's third-largest river, and by the Kwando, which also flows down from Angola, twice changing its name – first to Linyanti and then to Chobe – on its way to join the mighty Zambezi 70 kilometres upstream from the Victoria Falls.

The Linyanti-Chobe has its fertile floodplain, and the swamplands of the far northern region are magical in their moist lushness. But the Okavango system is very much larger, its impact on the Kalahari countryside far more dramatic. The river, known as the Kubango in its upper (Angolan) reaches, negotiates Namibia's Caprivi region and runs down through a narrow, 100-km-long panhandle before fanning out into a magnificent wetland delta that, at peak flood, is almost 15 000 square kilo-

metres in extent. The Okavango Delta's waters occasionally flow south to feed historic Lake Ngami and north-east to the game-rich Mababe Depression, but its principal (though still low-volume and very sporadic) outlet is eastwards, to the plains, pans and vegetated 'islands' of the northern Kalahari's Makgadikgadi basin.

Rocks and minerals

Beneath the great mantle of wind-blown Kalahari sandveld lies some of the world's oldest material: a number of the granite gneisses in the eastern region of Botswana were formed over 3 500 million years ago, which is not all that long on the geological calendar, after Planet Earth itself began to cool. More common, though, are the much younger (300-million-year-old) Karoo deposits – basalt lavas, sandstones, shales (clays), thin seams of coal – which underlie about half the country's surface.

Even more recent are the kimberlites, narrow 'pipes' of molten material thrust up from the earth's core by volcanic action 80 million years ago. In a few instances the high temperatures and pressures created by these massive forces transformed the carbon contained in the lava into diamonds which, after their discovery a little over two decades ago, have provided the impetus for an economic miracle. Among other minerals locked into the geological formations are copper and nickel (mined at Selebi-Phikwe), the gold and copper-silver deposits of the Francistown and Matsitama areas, manganese and iron ore, and rich coal reserves near Morapule and Serowe in the east. The pans of the north-central Kalahari yield salt, potash and soda-ash.

The climatic pattern

Botswana's climate is classed as 'continental tropical', though apart from the far-northern areas very little of the country has that steamy lushness one usually associates with the latter word. The wet season, such as it is, straddles the summer period, the first rains falling (in good years) towards the end of October and the last ones in March. Occasionally the season persists into April and even May; during December and January, the wettest months, rainstorms begin to build up from about midday to produce brief late-afternoon downpours that are often accompanied by thunder and lightning of Olympian proportions.

That is the typical pattern but by no means an unvarying one. The rains are unreliable; often they're late, and there can be days, even weeks on end when the summer skies remain clear; all too often the land, its farmers and their livestock suffer droughts that periodically create national crises – in three dry years during the mid-1980s, for example, more than a million head of cattle perished from lack of water.

The country, for most of the year, is virtually wind-free, but early in August a hot breeze begins to blow, sweeping Kalahari sand across the entire country. Then, two months later, the rains come. Average precipitation is a fairly healthy 475 millimetres, but the figure is deceptive: much of the moisture is lost through evaporation. The north-eastern areas get a lot more rain (about 650 millimetres a year) than the arid southern and southwestern regions, some parts of which average around 250 millimetres, others even less.

Summer days are hot, suffocatingly so in the weeks that precede the coming of the cooling rains, and shade temperatures rise to the 38 °C mark and higher, reaching a blistering 44 °C on rare occasions. Winters are clear-skied and bone-dry, the air seductively warm during the daylight hours but, because there's no cloud cover, cold at night and in the early mornings. Sometimes bitterly so: frost is common; small quantities of water can freeze, and snow has been known to fall in the Kalahari.

For tourists, the best visiting months are from April through to October – in terms of both weather and game-viewing. It is during this period that the wildlife of the great spaces gathers around what water there is – the natural waterholes and the borehole-fed dams – and are at their most visible. The plains game, though – gemsbok and eland, springbok and hartebeest – have adapted in remarkable fashion to drought conditions and don't need standing water in order to survive.

Plants and animals

Driving through the vast interior of Botswana, one is struck by the unrelenting sameness of the landscapes – mile after unchanging mile of level, sun-blasted, monochromatic countryside scantily clad by grass and scrub and the occasional stand of trees clinging tenaciously to the sandy soil.

Vegetation is determined largely by rainfall patterns; the ground cover becomes progressively thicker as you travel north. Around 90 per cent of the country is classed as savanna – bush savanna in the south-west, sparsely wooded tree savanna in much of the remainder. Even in the moister east the river reaches, notably those of the Shashe, the Motloutse and the Mhalatswe, have been largely denuded of their once rich vegetation by overgrazing and by the voraciousness of shifting agriculture. True forests are found only in the far north, along the banks of the Chobe River, and even these are not of the close canopy type.

The dominant woodland species in the south and central regions is acacia in its several forms – camelthorn, blackthorn

and others – though the inhospitable central Kalahari sandveld also manages to sustain the morukuru, or tamboti (*Spirostachys africanus*), a hardy, deciduous species that is informally known as the jumping bean tree (its fruit is often attacked by an insect, whose larva develops in the seed-pod and, through its convulsions, causes the pod to leap a few centimetres into the air – a sight only for sober eyes). In the more kindly north, though, the acacia gives way to handsome ironwood (mopane), silver leaf (mogonono), Zimbabwean teak (mokusi), wild almond (mongongo), to marula and, notably on the northern fringes of the Makgadikgadi pans, to the bizarre baobab.

Some of these trees have value as well as interest. Locals consider the mopane worm a prized delicacy, and the caterpillars are collected by the sackful to be dried in the sun and then either roasted, fried, eaten raw or exported to South Africa. Mongongo nuts have succulent kernels that provide the Bushmen of the north-west with their staple diet for much of the year. Mokusi and, to a lesser extent, mopane are commercially logged; villagers use the soft wood of the marula in the crafting of bowls, plates and musical drums. The yellow, edible marula fruit, which ripens between April

A welcome sight after the long dry months of winter – rainclouds gather over the Savute flats in the Chobe National Park at the start of summer, a portent of the few good months to come.

and June, is much sought after by the rural Tswana: the protein-rich nuts are usually cooked with porridge, and the bark reputedly has anti-malarial and other medicinal properties. Baboons and monkeys and, according to legend, elephants too, are also fond of the marula – sometimes, it is said, rather too fond: they become happily inebriated after eating the overripe, fermenting fruit that lies on the ground – or so the story goes.

The Okavango Delta, though embraced by semi-desert on all sides, is in an entirely different botanical category. Its channels are edged by dense beds of reeds, its lovely lagoons graced by water lilies and its islands by tall palms. Oddly enough some of the dryland, drought-resistant species – lofty acacias, sausage and leadwood trees among others – also thrive in this most magnificent of wetlands.

The great sandy spaces of the central and southern interior, despite the bleakness of the landscapes, do have their occasional and modest floral beauty. In springtime, just before the onset of the wet season, the acacia trees become bright with yellow and white blooms, and when the rare rains do fall the ground plants – crimson lilies and wild hibiscus, acanthus, amocharis and many others – bring a little colour to the desolate land. The blossoms are short-lived, many are infrequent: the lilies flower for less than four days, the vellozias only once every three or four years.

The hardy desert succulents are remarkable for the ingenious way they have adapted to their harsh environment – and, some of them, for their capacity to provide man and animal with sustenance. More that two hundred thirstland species are classed as edible, among them the protein-rich and most tasty desert truffle, or legopo, which is gathered in quantity by the Bushmen to be sold, at a surprisingly high price, to the villagers of Ghanzi and other small, remote centres. Best known and most valuable of the plants, though, are the tsamma melon (*Citrullus lanatus*) and the wild cucumber (family Cucurbitaceae), harvested for the water they contain as well as for food. The tsamma,

indeed, has been essential to the survival of the Bushmen in some of the harsher sandveld areas; the fruits last for months after the parent plant has withered and, during the long dry months, they provided these desert people with their principal source of moisture. The seeds, too, are put to good use: they are collected, roasted, and then pounded into a kind of meal.

These plants of the wilderness also help sustain a surprisingly prolific and diverse wildlife complement that includes springbok, hartebeest, gemsbok (oryx), eland and a host of other, smaller animals, together with such carnivores as lion, caracal, serval and jackal. Many of the species, like the plants that nurture them, are superbly adapted to their near-waterless habitats.

The game populations are better provided for and more varied – and more accessible to the ordinary traveller – in the northern regions, notably in the Moremi game reserve and the magnificent Chobe National Park. Here, most of the better-known of the larger mammals are represented, and the bird life, especially in and around the wetlands, is quite remarkable for its diversity and beauty. Botswana's wildlife heritage is covered in more detail further on, between pages 34 and 39.

Even in the harsh thirstland of the Central Kalahari springtime brings relief, here evident in the bright yellow blossoms and waxy green seedpods of an acacia.

THE PEOPLE

Botswana has a total population of just under 1,4 million (1993 estimate), over 80 per cent of which is concentrated in the better-watered, more fertile eastern regions – those that border on South Africa and Zimbabwe. The annual growth rate, at around 3,4 per cent, is among the highest in the world; over half the population is under the age of 16 years.

Most Batswana (the collective name for the country's inhabitants) depend in one way or another on the land for a living, but as in nearly every other developing country 'urban drift', the migration of families from the rural areas, is enlarging the towns and swelling the ranks of the unemployed. In the early 1990s rather more than a quarter of the country's population lived in an urban environment.

A phenomenon peculiar (though not exclusive) to Botswana is the unusually large traditional 'village' whose residents can number anything up to 40 000 and which functions as the principal residential centre – in effect the capital – of the tribal grouping. Most of the inhabitants are involved in or otherwise depend on stockfarming even though the villages may be far from the communal grazing lands: outlying cattle posts give shelter to the herdsmen and provide watering points for their cattle. The average farmer, or pastoralist, will usually spend part of each week at these remote and rudimentary little places, returning to his family in the central village for frequent but brief 'weekends'. The wealthier cattlemen own a large number of these posts, which are widely spread over the immensity of the grassland plains and separated from each other by anything up to 100 kilometres of featureless terrain. Many of the villagers, moreover, run second homes in the cultivated lands nearby.

That, in brief, is the basic structure of traditional society in much of Botswana, though the pattern is by no means rigid and indeed the system is subject to erosion as young people progressively move to the towns, and older ones leave the central village to set up homes on their lands and at the cattle posts.

More than half the people of Botswana are of Tswana origin and the remainder heavily influenced by if not absorbed into Tswana culture. The word Tswana, in fact, is a fairly loose generic classification that embraces, within the country's borders, ten or twelve major groupings. It also encompasses the nearly two million people of South Africa's Bophuthatswana region, and many more who live in South Africa's northern industrial centres. The Tswana are historically related to the Sotho peoples of the Transvaal and the Kingdom of Lesotho, and indeed are sometimes referred to as the Western Sotho.

Biggest of Botswana's Tswana groupings is the Bangwato, who make up about a quarter of the total population and are traditional overlords of about a fifth of the land (the tribal capital is Serowe, in the east), followed by the Bakwena and the Bangwaketse, who live in the Gaborone area. The smaller groups comprise the Bakgatla, the Bamalete and the Batlokwa, all of whom also inhabit the south-east; the Rolong (Barolong), straddling the border with South Africa, and the Batawana of the north-central (Ngami) and far-western border region.

Although interrelated, each of the groups has it own, traditional chiefs and enjoys proprietary rights over its own lands. Which is not to say, however, that the groups are homogeneous within themselves: on the contrary each has, over time and for complex historical reasons, assimilated other peoples of both Tswana and non-Tswana origin.

Among non-Tswana minority groupings are the Bakalanga, the Bakgalagadi, the Bayei, Hambukushu and Basubiya, and a 25 000-strong Ovaherero community which is a fairly recent addition to the country's demographic tapestry. There are also some 40 000 San (Bushmen), known locally as the Basarwa, nearly all of whom are semi-nomadic occupants of the southern, south-central and western semi-desert regions. The white population numbers some 15 000, two-thirds of whom are not citizens of Botswana.

The statistical picture shows a popula-

tion density of 2,7 per square kilometre across the board and huge regional disparities: 15 people a square kilometre in the south-east, and a density of just 0,2 in the arid Ghanzi and Kgalagadi districts of the west. Life expectancy at birth is around 53 years for males, 59 years for females, and rising; the birth rate is 44 per 1 000 population; infant mortality is about 90 per 1 000 population but this is declining.

Botswana's principal language is Setswana and its various dialects; Setswana and English are the official means of communication; nearly all townsmen speak passable and some speak excellent English.

The traditional Tswana

The body of oral history, coloured by legend and perhaps by myth as well, tells us that the Tswana's ancestry goes back to Malope, of the Kwena dynasty and descendant of Mogale, who ruled the area to the west of today's Pretoria (the lovely Magaliesberg range of hills derives its name from 'Mogale's Mountains') in the mid-14th century. A son of Malope is thought to have gath-

ered a following and moved off into the Zeerust area of the western Transvaal, his group eventually fragmentating. The offshoots moved off, some merging with other Sotho-speaking peoples, others remaining independent, still others eventually rejoining their parent group.

Fission, migration and fusion are constant (and, to the Eurocentric observer, highly confusing) elements in Tswana society. The offspring of chiefs did not customarily fight for succession and control but were inclined to break away from the main body to form new tribes. But at the same time there were also powerful counter-forces that favoured integration: wealth and status flowed from the ownership of cattle, and those groups poorly endowed with livestock tended to gravitate towards and, in many cases, allow themselves to be absorbed by the richer communities. Hence the endless process of fragmentation and amalgamation that characterizes the story of the Tswana.

However that may be, the basic Tswana structures have to a notable extent survived in the rural areas; most country families still work, live and relate

Serowe, tribal capital of the Bangwato people, is also the home village of the late Sir Seretse Khama, founding father of the modern Republic of Botswana.

to each other very much as their forefathers did.

The traditional Tswana political system can be described as a village democracy. Each community is divided into wards called *dikgotla*, each with its open space, or *kgotla*, in which meetings are held, village affairs debated and disputes settled. The local chief (or, perhaps more correctly, subchief) also has his *kgotla*, a grander affair invariably sited in the centre of the village. Shared amenities include school, store, clinic or dispensary, and water taps, though in the larger villages the individual wards often boast their own boreholes. Within the wards, too, the nuclear families (individual households) have their own courtyards enclosing living quarters and a granary.

Smaller, outlying villages maintain close relations with the group capital, location of the royal *kgotla* and historic seat of the tribal government. In pre-independence days the latter was embodied in the person of the paramount chief, a man described by the late author and academic Isaac Schapera as 'the symbol of tribal unity, the central figure around whom tribal life revolves. He is at once ruler, judge, maker and guardian of the law, repository of wealth, dispenser of gifts, leader

in war, priest and magician of the peple'.

The chief was not, however, a straightforward authoritarian: he had strict obligations; he held the group's lands and other assets in trust and used them on behalf and to the benefit of his people; he made decisions with the help of his senior relatives, headmen and officials, and matters of important public policy were usually decided at a general council open to all adult male members of the group. The Tswana value honesty and outspokenness, and it was not unusual and quite acceptable for the chief to be opposed, even criticized, at these meetings.

The social order within the traditional communities was (and to a great degree still is) intricate. Seniority was clearly defined (the hierarchy extended down from the chief through an aristocracy of his kinsmen to commoners and, finally, to those who could be described as 'immigrants', or 'clients', people who had been assimilated but did not yet properly belong to the group). Tswana society is patrilineal: it is the eldest son of the senior (though not necessarily the first) wife who inherits. The question of affiliation, however, is complex. A person will, naturally, maintain close identification with the family *kgotla*, but there are also age groups or 'regiments' that cut

right across ward and kinship loyalties. This is a throwback to the old days, when physical defence was often of overriding moment to the groups, and young men were periodically drafted into service. Call-ups occurred every four years or so; initiation into the age-graded set involved a number of elaborate and in some instances painful ceremonies. For boys, the most important of these was circumcision and a period of seclusion, out in the veld some distance from the village, during which they endured a series of hardship trials and were taught the ways of the tribe. Girls also came together in sets to learn the secrets of womanhood and domesticity.

There is still an elaborate hierarchical structure within the traditional community, though now not nearly so well defined as it was in the earlier, more warlike days of inter-tribal rivalry and competition for the best grazing areas. Occupation of land and ownership of cattle were the criteria of rank; those who were conquered relinquished their livestock and either departed or, as mentioned, stayed to become absorbed as 'clients'. Again, time and political circumstance have eroded the social distinctions.

The majority of Tswana are nominal and about a third are practising Christians. Traditional belief, which embraces among other elements a Supreme Being, *Modimo*, and the influence of ancestral spirits (*badimo*), wilted before the onslaught of 19th-century European missionary zeal, and a lot of what was once sacred – certainly much of the body of elaborate ritual – has been abandoned. No longer, for instance, do young boys and girls go through the complex ceremony of initiation; rarely will you witness the ancient rites of rain-making or the mysterious process by which tribal boundaries are rendered inviolate.

The smaller groupings
Of the minority communities, the Kalanga are (probably) the largest, occupying much of the territory around Francistown, the Nata River in the north-east and, in much greater numbers, the south-western parts of neigh-

The village kgotla *is at the centre of Botswana's traditional political system, best described as village democracy. Here the tribal elders hear complaints, disputes and debate village affairs at the Serowe* kgotla, *historic seat of tribal government.*

bouring Zimbabwe. Small communities – the Kalanga were scattered far and wide during the tribal conflicts of the early 19th century – are to be found in several other parts of Botswana.

Little is known for certain about Kalanga origins, but similarities in the realms of language and spiritual conviction indicate that they are related to the ancient Karanga-Rozwi, builders of the remarkable citadel of Great Zimbabwe and rulers of an empire that, at its height in the 15th century, stretched from today's Botswana east to the Indian Ocean. More specifically, the Kalanga were almost certainly citizens of Butua, the state centred around Khame near modern Bulawayo. During the following three centuries the empire was riven by dynastic rivalry and more or less disintegrated, though the powerful Rosvi group were able to maintain a vague kind of authority over much of what is now Zimbabwe and northern Botswana until, in the early 1800s, it finally collapsed in the face of successive incursions by Nguni 'raiding kingdoms' from the south.

The south-western segment of the Rosvi domain embraced the Nyai people, who are thought to be the ancestors of today's Kalanga. Or rather, of the 'true' Kalanga because, over the

turbulent and often drought-stricken decades other groups – some from as far afield as western Zambia to the north and, even more distant, from the Drakensberg far to the east – settled among and were gradually absorbed by the main body of the group.

Threatened by the Ndebele incursions of the 1840s, some Kalanga placed themselves under the protection of the Ngwato group of the Tswana, a move that demoted their chiefs and eroded their distinctive tribal identity. Nevertheless, much remains of the ancestral past, including a residue of religious belief, which centred on the great oracle Mwari (known as Ngwale among the Kalanga). More significantly, and in marked contrast to the majority of Tswana, the Kalanga have a value system based on land rights. They are tillers of the earth who live in small communities. Although they do keep cattle and goats, livestock is valued more for its socially functional and religious relevance than as a symbol of wealth and prestige: cattle are used to placate the ancestral spirits, to pay the bride-price and as a reward from the chief to deserving individuals.

Adding a colourful touch to Botswana's human fabric are the 25 000 or

so Mbanderu – cousins to the Herero people – living in the Ngami lake region, to the south of the Okavango swamplands. Most of these proud and independent folk are descendants of groups who fled Namibia during the brutal Nama wars of the later 19th century and, more notably, after the German colonial conquest of the 1890s. The Herero of what was then known as German South West Africa bitterly resented white encroachment and all that it brought – alien laws and taxes, loss of land and of the age-old rights to common pastures and water resources – and in 1904 they rose in revolt. In doing so they triggered perhaps the bloodiest chapter in the annals of African colonial history. The rebellion lasted almost four years and in the end, after 88 savage military engagements, led to the extermination of three-quarters of the Herero nation: some 65 000 died during the convulsions, most of them of hunger and thirst in the barren wastes of eastern Namibia. A few escaped across the desert into present-day Botswana, seeking and, the lucky ones, finding kinsfolk who had fled the earlier troubles.

Initially the newcomers lived as servants of the local Tswana, from whom they learnt to cultivate the unpromising soil, but soon enough they reverted to

A goatherd drives his flock along a track near Rakops in the central Kalahari region. Most Batswana own cattle and goats, valued more for their social significance than as a source of food or income.

their traditional pastoral ways and began accumulating livestock. By the mid-1930s they were collectively rich enough to cut the bonds of servitude and are now among the country's more prosperous cattle-ranchers. In visual terms the most remarkable Herero characteristic is the 'traditional' costume worn by the women: a long, Victorian-type dress adapted from the styles favoured by the wives of the early European missionaries in Namibia.

Culturally distinct, too, are three small groups who live on the floodplains of the Okavango and Chobe – the Basubiya, Bayei and Hambukushu (see page 40). These were and many of them still are river people, skilled fishermen and hunters by tradition but they are also cultivators and, to a limited extent, keepers of cattle, which are used chiefly as pack animals.

Parts of the semi-desert region and its fringes are home to small communities known as Kgalagadi (the word from which Kalahari is derived), historically a scattered and generally poor people who subsisted on the fruits of the hunt, on their gleanings of wild plants, on the modest crops of sorghum and beans they managed to grow and the few goats they kept. Some Kgalagadi, however – mainly those who have taken to ranching – now rank among Botswana's wealthier families; many more are moderately prosperous wage-earners.

More closely associated with the

Herero women in Maun make a colourful spectacle in their 'traditional' costumes – Victorian style dress adapted from that favoured by the wives of early European missionaries.

This stylized zebra, one of several thousand rock paintings at Tsodilo Hills in north-western Botswana, has been adopted as the symbol of the National Museum.

desert are the San, or Bushmen, earliest of Southern Africa's inhabitants: long before the arrival of either the Bantu-speaking migrants from the north and the white settlers from across the seas, small bands of mobile hunter-gatherers roamed the great sunlit spaces in search of sustenance and solitude, a unique culture once dominant in the vast area that extended from the Atlantic to the Indian Ocean and from East Africa down to the southern coast.

Not that the word 'dominant', and all that it suggests, is appropriate in the context of San culture. Entirely without malice or hostility, these gentle, remarkable people had (and still have) a profound belief in sharing: in co-operation within the family, between group and group, between humankind and the environment. Custom and conviction excluded personal hostility; nature, both animate and inanimate, was sanctified, hallowed in the mystic rituals of the hunt and the entranced dance, and in the lively rock-paintings and engravings that grace some thousands of sites throughout the subcontinent.

Some of this art can be seen in, among other places, the rugged Tsodilo Hills that rise above the sand-dunes of Botswana's lonely north-western region

(see page 18). Their creators, the greatest of all prehistoric artists, employed surprisingly advanced foreshortening techniques, a three-dimensional approach that gave vibrant reality to the hunt; movement, flow, power are all there in the leap of an antelope, in the surge of a buffalo. The colours, too, were striking (many of the subjects have now faded; time, weather and, more recently, vandalism have all taken their toll), their essence the mineral oxides of the earth – manganese for black, clay for white, haematite to produce the deep browns, the reds and the yellows.

The San could not compete with the more territorial, warlike pastoral Bantu-speaking peoples who, from about the middle of the first millennium, began to encroach on the ancient hunting grounds. Some of the groups were assimilated by the newcomers (who added nine of the San 'click' sounds into their own Nguni languages), others remained in the most inhospitable of the regions – the remote wildernesses of the north-western Cape, Namibia, and the Kalahari sands of Botswana.

Until very recently the true desert San lived, and a very few still live, much as their ancestors did, moving in small groups, each with its defined territory.

The women gathered roots and edible berries and wild melons (a source, as we've seen, of water as well as food); the men hunted with a wooden bow strung with sinew, and arrows which they carried in a skin or bark quiver (though they also used spears and clubs, as the occasion demanded). The arrowheads were tipped with poison made from insect grubs or from certain plants – toxins that acted slowly on the prey's nervous system, and invariably the hunters had to follow the animal for a fair distance before it weakened.

When the kill was made, the whole clan joined in the feast, singing, and dancing to an aeons-old choreography around the night-time fire.

Meat, though, was an occasional bonus rather than a dietary staple. When game was scarce, which it most often was, the group divided into smaller parties to range far and wide over the sandveld terrain, garnering the plants of the desert and its insects, snakes, lizards. In especially dry areas, and elsewhere in times of drought, the San stored water in ostrich shells, which they buried in remote and apparently featureless places deep beneath the sandy surface, and were able to locate again with uncanny accuracy even when no signs of the cache were visible. Ostrich shell was also used for personal ornamentation; traditional clothing comprised skin karosses, loincloths and aprons. Possessions were few and simple: nothing was owned that could not be carried. Similarly, shelters were rudimentary, the stick structures abandoned when the group moved on.

Today, Botswana's San have been forced to relinquish the nomadic lifestyle in favour of a more settled life.

The country's population also embraces small numbers of Nama (originally from Namibia) and mixed-descent (Afro-European) people, and some 15 000 white residents, technically skilled for the most part, many of them on contract to government agencies or local business enterprises, a goodly number involved in the burgeoning tourism sector.

A young Zhu boy peers wide-eyed throught the photographer's camera lens. He and his grandmother are members of a small settlement of San people still residing at Tsodilo Hills,

FOCAL POINTS

Apart from its capital, Botswana has no cities in the generally accepted sense of the word; its other centres, concentrated along the eastern border, are modest enough even by African standards, the largest perhaps comparable in size to a middle-ranking English or American country town. Some of the larger places, though fairly substantial in terms of population, are essentially villages in the traditional mould, unsophisticated, boasting few of the luxuries and conveniences associated with modern living. Nevertheless, each has its own story, its distinctive character, its unique position in the history and culture of the region.

Gaborone
The country's seat of government, known as Gaberones until fairly recently and named after a long-living Tlokwa chief, started life in the 1890s, first as an administrative centre and then a railway halt on the long and lonely line linking South Africa's Cape province with the Rhodesian (now Zimbabwean) town of Bulawayo. In fact the settlement goes back a further ten years: the original tribal headquarters, Tlokweng, was built in 1881 on the banks of the Ngotwane River four kilometres away. The administrative centre is now the site of a city suburb (nostalgically called The Village).

Gaborone functioned as the headquarters of the country's southern province (there were only two provincial divisions during the colonial era) until the run-up to independence in 1966, when it replaced Mafikeng (formerly Mafeking of Anglo-Boer War siege fame; the town lies outside Botswana's borders) as the national capital. The move heralded a dramatic transformation: over the next quarter-century the place grew from a tiny settlement with some 6 000 residents into a handsome little metropolis with a population of around 145 000.

The planners started virtually from scratch, laying out the spacious town on level ground garlanded by attractive trees; among the town centre's more notable features are The Mall, a pedestrian thoroughfare and adjoining square flanked by shops, the prestigious President Hotel, banks, office blocks, embassies. At the eastern end are the municipal buildings, the public library, and the magnificent National Museum and Art Gallery (exhibits include impressive painted dioramas and mounted animals); the western end is graced by the National Assembly chambers and the city's rather lovely public park. Other landmarks are the University of Botswana and the national sports stadium and, to the north of town, the Seretse Khama international airport.

Gaborone has been adjudged by the prestigious British monthly business periodical *Corporate Location* as one of the 'Cities of the Future'. In 1993 the magazine ranked Johannesburg fourth among cities with potential, linking the South African metropolis to Gaborone (which it placed fourth on a separate list of 'movers and shakers' among the smaller, up-and-coming centres) and Namibia's Windhoek in a 'triangle of growth' that, with the help of a new highway that will soon connect the three, may well transform the character of south-central Africa. In 1994 American diplomats voted Gaborone among the most pleasant of postings.

The city is well served by hotels, prominent among them the luxurious Gaborone Sun, which incorporates a lively casino, two restuarants (Giovannis' has a dance band and nightly cabaret), 40 or so executive suites among its 200-plus rooms; the Sheraton (200 rooms, including the upmarket Towers units, and a well-appointed business centre); the imposing Cresta President and its two sister hotels, the rather more budget-orientated Cresta Gaborone and Cresta Lodge. Four kilometres out of town is the Oasis Motel, a pleasantly peaceful venue of self-contained chalets and a restaurant known for its excellent Botswana beef and (somewhat surprisingly) its seafood.

Of interest to visitors in and around town are:
• The ruins of the early Kolobeng mission station, the country's first Christian church, located half-an-hour's drive out on the Thamega road.
• Village craft industries at the Pelegano Centre (pottery, decorated gourds); Mokolodi (15 kilometres from Gaborone; ceramic and carved-bone jewellery, printed fabrics), and Odi village (18 kilometres; woven tapestries, mats, blankets, jerseys).
• Gaborone dam (for yachting, windsurfing and fishing enthusiasts).
• Gaborone game reserve, the St Clair lion park and the outstanding Mokolodi nature reserve.

Francistown

Strategically located astride the main road and rail lines of communication into both Zimbabwe and Zambia, Francistown is the country's second largest and most industrialized urban centre. The town – a rather down-to-earth place that, in visual terms, has little to commend it – has its origins in the gold fever that infected early European hunters and the South African and Australian prospectors who followed them: the area around the Dati River had been worked extensively and apparently very profitably by the old Karangan communities, whose long-abandoned shafts and adits spoke volumes to the newcomers, hinting of King Solomon and the fabulous land of Ophir. Later a fairly substantial mine (the Monarch) and its attendant town were established and thrived in rowdy fashion for a while during the 1890s, but the Dati fields never lived up to the dreams of the diggers (one of whom, Daniel Francis, bequeathed his name to the settlement): most of the easily accessible gold had been extracted by the ancients and much of what remained lay far beneath the ground, well beyond the capability of late-19th century mining techniques.

The town, established after this initial disappointment, derived moderate prosperity from the lone gold-mine and its position on the major north-south overland route and its status as administrative centre for the territory's northern region. The Monarch mine limped along until its closure in 1964, but other minerals, notably copper and nickel, have been discovered in the area. Francistown now has a population of around 70 000, and its manufacturing sector encompasses textiles, knitwear, plastics, shoes and related accessories.

The town also serves as a major stopover for visitors on their way to the game-rich Chobe and Moremi reserves and the Okavango Delta; among its hotels are the very pleasant and comfortably appointed Cresta Thapama (excellent health and fitness facilities; pool; two restaurants; two bars) and the Marang which offers both family chalets and standard rooms.

Francistown is Botswana's second largest urban centre and the country's industrial capital.

Maun

The administrative headquarters of Ngamiland, Maun (pronounced 'Ma-oong') meaning 'the place of the reeds', is the cheerfully animated hub of Botswana's tourism industry, a jumping-off point for journeys to the Okavango swamplands and the Moremi game reserve to the north, and to the great sandveld wildernesses of the south.

Until recently a sleepy, dusty, sun-drenched, goat- and donkey-infested little settlement, the town has expanded in spectacular fashion over the past few years: it is still shaded by lovely riverine trees, the goats and donkeys still wander at will, but the central streets are now tarred and alive with Mercs and brand-new four-by-fours and a milling throng of outward-bound humanity (nearly everyone seems to be on his way somewhere) and construction companies are busily changing the skyline. Maun airport has an impressive new terminal complex and its runway has been upgraded to accommodate large jet aircraft; the macadamized highway from Francistown and Nata is now complete, and that leading north-west through Shakawe to Namibia's Caprivi region is virtually so.

Maun's social scene is lively and informal, its twin focuses now, as always, Riley's Hotel and The Duck Inn. The former was taken over and renovated fairly recently by the respected Cresta hospitality group, but something of the old, relaxed colonial days comes across in its wide riverside verandah. The Duck Inn is a place where you meet characters who seem to have stepped straight from the set of *The African Queen*.

A large number of safari firms are either based or represented in Maun, together with an array of ancillary services: here one can organize an Okavango lodge holiday or a mobile safari, a game-viewing, birding, fishing or hunting expedition; hire a Land-Rover or powerboat, charter an aircraft. In town are banks, service stations, shops that sell curios, fabric, liquor, fresh produce and pretty well everything you could possibly need for your wilderness holiday, from a bush-jacket to an inflatable canoe.

The town of Maun, gateway to the Okavango, has shown remarkable growth in recent years. Today there are paved roads and streetlighting where once dusty dirt tracks sufficed.

Maun is on the banks of the Thamalakane River, whose clear, often lily-covered waters sustain a great many fish as well as hippo, crocodile and a marvellous parade of birds. It is also a playground for the angler, the canoeist and for those who choose to explore its attractive reaches by *mokoro*, the traditional African dug-out craft. North of town, also on the Thamalakane, is the old-established and charming Crocodile Camp (see page 41).

Lake Ngami

About 70 kilometres to the south-west of Maun lies one of the more mysterious of Africa's physical features. Ngami was once, not too long ago, a substantial, permanent, ice-blue sheet of water, 45 by 16 kilometres in extent, located rather incongruously in the sandy, scantily clad grasslands to the south of the Okavango Delta, a magnet for early European explorers such as Andersson, Galton and the admirable David Livingstone. Word of a great inland sea – what the San (Bushmen) knew as 'the

place of giraffes' and the Yei people as 'the place of reeds' – had percolated through to the white travelling fraternity well before the 1850s. Livingstone, accompanied by William Oswell and Mungo Murray, made his way to its shores, by the conventional northern route, in 1849, but it is Charles Andersson's expedition that is most celebrated in the annals. Determined to 'fill the empty spaces on the map between the northern Cape and Portuguese settlement (Angola) in the west', he negotiated the wild, heat-blasted immensity of the Namibian wastelands in 1853 to reach the lake from the west – an epic journey indeed.

Ngami, which relies on sporadic overspill from the Delta and thus, ultimately, on the rains that fall in the Angolan highlands far to the north-west, remains dry for long periods – a flat, featureless, dusty plain that cannot support life. When it is full, though, it's two metres deep and home to a myriad aquatic birds – storks and flamingoes, gulls, herons and colonies of breeding pelicans

– and to a prolific fish population. At these times the Tswana and the colourfully garbed Herero pastoralists of the region bring their herds to the shores, and the Bayei fishermen prosper.

Tsodilo Hills

Rising over 400 metres above the empty Kalahari sandveld of the northwest, 400 kilometres from Maun, is a long ridge of ochre-coloured quartzite heights (there are four major segments) that the renowned author Laurens van der Post termed the 'mountain of the gods'. These are the Tsodilo Hills, home to man a full 80 000 years ago, though it is the legacy of later peoples that catch the eye and stir the imagination.

To generations of San (Bushmen), this was sacred ground, and they used its rocks and overhangs as canvasses for their marvellous art. More than 3 500 of their paintings have survived, many of quite outstanding quality, the majority on the so-called Female hill (there's also a Male and a Child; the fourth has no name). The oldest of the paintings is believed to date back some 4 000 years and is simple in style and content; later ones depict more complex subjects – collections of animals and so on.

San communities still inhabit the area, and some individuals will hire themselves out as guides, but they seem to have lost touch with the distant past and can tell you little or nothing of their artistic forerunners and their lifestyle.

Drotsky's Caves

Some 150 kilometres west of the Okavango Delta, in the desolate dunelands close to the Namibian border, is a series of splendid and in parts beautiful dolomite chambers and passageways known locally as the Gcwahaba (the !Kung Bushman's name for 'the hyaena's lair') caverns and to the wider world as Drotsky's Caves (Bushmen revealed their presence to a farmer called Drotsky in the 1930s). They are remarkable for their spaciousness, and the size and number of their stalactites – descending flowstone formations, some of which exceed six metres in length. The stalagmites are also prominent. The complex, on the dust-dry

The Tsodilo Hills, 'micaceous quartzite schist' inselbergs, rise dramatically from the featureless surrounding Kalahari sandveld in north-west Botswana. More than 3 500 examples of rock art have been identified in the hills.

banks of the Gcwahaba Valley, are a source of endless fascination to geologists and climatologists, their convolutions of eroded rock providing an insight into the moist and dry periods of the region's past (the last wet spell, it is thought, occurred between 2 000 and 1 500 years ago).

The caves are open to the general public (there are two entrances) but extreme caution is urged on would-be explorers: there are no visitor facilities, either *en route* along the rough access track or at the site itself, and it is pitch dark inside the labyrinth. So unless you come well prepared – with a minimum two days' supply of provisions and water, plenty of reserve fuel and, most important, lighting (flashlight or gas lamp) to find your way around – you'll be inviting danger as well as discomfort.

Lobatse

This little centre lies 70 kilometres to the south of Gaborone and close to South Africa's Bophuthatswana region, a strategic position that once promoted growth, but shortage of water has retarded economic development. The setting – in a valley flanked by rocky hills – is attractive, Lobatse rather less so, likened by travel writer T.V. Bulpin

to 'a slovenly but animated cow town of the Wild West'. Indeed livestock is much in evidence: the place has a busy abattoir and one of Africa's largest meatprocessing plants; cattle from the surrounding ranchlands and from the Ghanzi district, way across the vast interior plains, arrive on the hoof, in their thousands, to be slaughtered.

Lobatse is Botswana's judicial capital, seat of the High Court and headquarters of the geological survey department. The courthouse once – before Gaborone became the capital city – served as the territory's Legislative Council chamber. The town has an airfield, several garages, and the Cresta Cumberland Hotel, one of Botswana's most attractive hostelries (swimming pool, landscaped grounds, excellent à la carte restaurant).

Jwaneng

Located in the semi-desert 120 kilometres west of the Gaborone-Lobatse axis is the little town of Jwaneng, once a scruffy little cattle post but now a richly flourishing centre of the Botswana diamond industry.

A major new diamond pipe was discovered in the area during the late 1970s and the Jwaneng mine came into full production in June 1982 to give a powerful impetus to the country's export performance: initial annual output was estimated at about 4,4 million carats but the pipe has exceeded all expectations, yielding a yearly 9 million carats by the end of the 1980s. Around a third of Jwaneng's diamonds are of gem quality – a highly gratifying proportion by any standards.

The town has an airfield, modern shops and, predictably, excellent sporting facilities.

Serowe

The capital of the Bangwato group and birthplace of Sir Seretse Khama, the country's first president, Serowe is the largest of the Tswana tribal 'villages' (see page 12) – its population is estimated at around 50 000 – and arguably the most attractive. For the most part it comprises clusters of circular, thatched, traditional Tswana homes each encircled by spacious courtyard and garden, the whole set beneath a tree-mantled hill surrounded, in turn, by cultivated lands and, beyond, great expanses of grazing country.

The term 'village', though, is somewhat misleading: Serowe is well developed, boasting modern government buildings, shops, two small hotels, the splendid Sekgoma Memorial Hospital, and a tarred road that leads to the main highway. At the base of the hill is the Khama III Memorial Museum, located in the Red House and containing memorabilia of the royal family together with displays of Ngwato and San culture. Khama III's grave is graced by bronze duiker antelope, the work of the celebrated South African sculptor Anton van Wouw. The hill, named Thathaganyane, is worth climbing for the views it offers and for the ruins of the 11th-century settlement at the top.

Selebi-Phikwe

With a population of close to 60 000, this the third largest of Botswana's towns, and one of the newest – it was founded in 1967, and named after two local cattle posts, when impressive reserves of copper and nickel were charted in the two areas. Both mine and town suffered initially from fluctuating and often poor world commodity prices, but the operating company (Roan Selection Trust) managed to weather the storm – and indeed to enlarge its investment, in the early 1990s, with the development of the high-grade Selebi North deposit.

Selebi-Phikwe is a modern, good-looking little centre of neat houses, shops, banks, a golf course and an expanding industrial base.

Kanye

Between Lobatse and Jwaneng is another large and picturesque village, similar to but not so generously endowed with modern amenities as Serowe. This is Kanye, principal centre of the Bangwaketsi group of the Tswana and originally a hilltop settlement; the name derives from *gokanya*, which means 'to strike down' or destroy and accurately describes its early function: the citadel had consistently if sporadically suffered attack ever since its founding by Makaba in the late 18th century, most seriously by Mzilikazi and his Ndebele raiders and, later, by the German adventurer Jan Bloem. Its natural defences were reinforced by stone walls; the summit accommodated the royal family and its wards, while the commoners inhabited the valley below.

The village, with a population of around 30 000, has changed little in character over the decades: on the slopes, Tswana-style homes – house, outbuildings, courtyard – cluster around the central meeting places, or *kgotla*; narrow alleyways meander in between; many of the walls are attractively decorated; the chief's residence is still sited atop the hill. In the valley, though, government buildings, schools, clinics and modern houses have made their appearance, and there's an airfield nearby. The wider area holds promising deposits of asbestos and manganese.

Mochudi

Another of Botswana's large traditional villages, Mochudi lies some 25 kilometres north of Gaborone, in an attractive setting of hills. Although fairly modern – it boasts a training college, primary and secondary schools, community centre, shops, some industry and an airstrip – it retains much of its timeless character. Of special interest are the splendid old Kgatla houses with sweeping expanses of thatched roofing that shade the circular verandahs. Many of the entrances are charmingly decorated; the chief's residence is sited on top of a hill known as Phuthadikobo; the local museum is notable for its handicraft displays.

Mahalapye and its neighbours

Both Mahalapye and Palapye, 70 kilometres along the railway line leading north, are named after the local rocks and the animals around them, most notably the teeming herds of impala antelope that once roamed the eastern grasslands. Each is an agricultural centre of some note; both have their modest scatter of shops, garages, hotels, airstrip. To the west of Mahalapye lies the old Ngwato capital of Shoshong, site of two early mission stations. The substantial Morupule coal mine is located close to Palapye.

The late Sir Seretse Khama, independent Botswana's first premier and a member of the Ngwato royal house.

The Orapa was the first of Botswana's thriving diamond mines. It was opened in 1971, and remains the backbone of the country's flourishing economy.

Orapa

The town – the first of Botswana's flourishing diamond centres – is located in the north-central interior, at the edge of the Kalahari and close to Ntwetwe Pan. Its giant kimberlite pipe was discovered by De Beers geologists in the late 1960s and the mine became operational in 1971, since when it has yielded a huge number of stones, though proportionally far fewer of gem quality than the newer Jwaneng mine (see above, page 19).

Orapa is a self-sufficient, beautifully run little place that has all the comforts and modern conveniences, including a modern shopping area, schools, hospital, two swimming pools, a golf course and a recreational dam. It remains, however, a 'closed' town, and visitors must obtain a permit before entering.

Kasane

Once a remote and entirely forgettable little village, Kasane's strategic location astride the main tourist routes has led to rapid expansion in recent years. The busy little town lies on the Chobe River in the far north-east of the region and offers trouble-free access to (and functions as administrative headquarters of) the splendid Chobe National Park, and

to two other tourist meccas: Namibia's Caprivi 'strip' to the west and the Victoria Falls on the Zimbabwe-Zambia border to the east. The road south to Nata, Francistown, Gaborone and points beyond is now fully tarred.

Kasane and its surrounds boast five hotels, a bank, supermarket, bakery, liquor store, and a fine new airport (it enjoys international status). It also boasts a majestic and ancient baobab tree with a whimsical story to tell: in the distant colonial past its hollowed-out trunk served as the local prison.

The Kalahari towns

There are precious few concentrations of population on the great plains of the Kalahari sandveld, and those that do exist are tiny, immensely remote settlements, most of which enjoy little more than a tenuous acquaintanceship with the modern world. Three of them, however, are rather special.

The biggest and among the most isolated is Ghanzi, a thriving little ranching centre located between the Central Kalahari Game Reserve and the Namibian border in the far west. The area is blessed with good pasturage, abundant underground and some surface water (from the limestone ridge),

and the cattle herds usually flourish.

Originally home to the San people, the area was occupied in the 1870s by a small party of Transvaal Boers led by the colourful if unappetizing Hendrik van Zyl. The settlers prospered (Van Zyl is said to have retained a hundred servants to look after his splendid homestead and its imported French furniture), but relations between the newcomers and the local Tswana deteriorated and, in due course, the white men were driven out. But other Boers followed, many of them members of the so-called Dorsland ('Thirstland') Trek on their way to a new promised land further north in Angola, and for a time Ghanzi functioned as a busy little staging post.

In the 1890s and again in the 1950s substantial land grants were awarded to immigrant families (in the former case as part of a campaign by Cecil Rhodes to impede German colonial expansion from the west), and Ghanzi took on the trappings of civilization. Today the village has administrative buildings, a number of stores, a hospital, petrol filling station and a hotel, the amiable Kalahari Arms (the village is a convenient stopover for the traveller between Maun and the Namibian capital of Windhoek).

Two other Kalahari towns are strategically situated on, or just off, the main tourist routes. Nata lies astride the road leading from Francistown to Kasane and the Chobe park to the north, and at its junction with the new westward highway to Maun and beyond. The 'village' – it comprises a couple of garages, a small store or two and a liquor outlet – is well placed for access to the Makgadikgadi and, to a lesser extent, the Nxai pans and serves as a convenient stopover on the way to the Okavango Delta; visitors stay at Nata Lodge, a pleasant oasis of thatched A-frame bungalows in a setting of monkeythorn, marula and palm trees close to Sowa Pan (see page 46).

The second centre, Gweta, is about 100 kilometres farther along the Maun road and it, too, provides a useful base for those intent on exploring the pans. Here there's a general dealer's store, a filling station and the Gweta Rest Camp, an inexpensive motel with restaurant, bar and curio shop.

PATTERNS OF THE PAST

The early story of Botswana – the movement of peoples and the establishment of settlement patterns – is a complex and, because there is precious little documentation, rather confusing narrative. Some of the highlights of the pre-colonial era are touched upon in the description of the various tribal groupings on pages 10 to 15.

Recorded history properly begins with the arrival in the general region of a succession of travellers, traders and men of God in the opening decade of the 19th century. The first to appear on the scene was Petrus Truter who, with William Somerville, was sent from Britain's Cape territory into the Tlhaping stronghold of Dithakong, then located 40 kilometres north of the Kuruman River and known at the time as Lattakoo (Tswana villages were periodically moved *en bloc* and renamed) to barter for cattle. They made contact with the Tlhaping in 1801, to be followed by other travellers, notably Hendrik van der Graaff and the German doctor and naturalist Martin Heinrich Lichtenstein (who collected and documented many species of animal and plant previously unknown to the scientific world) in 1805 and, a year later, by the artist and writer William Burchill. The latter recorded this and other journeys in his monumental *Travels in the Interior of Southern Africa*, describing with perception and sensitivity the peoples of the subcontinent and the region's rich and varied flora and fauna (when he eventually returned to England he took with him 40 000 botanical and thousands of insect specimens).

But all these were exploratory expeditions, temporary visitations that created little more than a ripple on the surface of Tswana traditional life. Far more enduring was the legacy of the Christian clerics who came soon after. Neither variety of visitor was active within the borders of today's Botswana (most of the events described took place well to the south), but they are nevertheless relevant to the country's early history – to the processes that led to colonial status and then to the creation of a modern state.

These men belong to one of the San (Bushman) communities of the central Kalahari. The Bushmen were the original inhabitants of what is today Botswana.

Men of God

In 1813 the London Missionary Society's (LMS) John Campbell, on an inspection tour of the organization's Southern African stations, made his way north across the Orange River into the land of the Tlhaping to be greeted warmly by Chief Mothibe, who invited him to 'send instructors and I will be a father to them'. The instructors, James Read and Robert Hamilton, duly arrived and set about their missionary work with patience and courage but, as it turned out, very little success. Read soon departed, leaving Hamilton to struggle along on his own for five long years. It became clear to the LMS that a much stonger personality was needed if the Christian message and the values it sought to impose were to penetrate this far frontier.

The man chosen was Robert Moffat, a Scotsman of humble origins (though he had trained as a horticulturist before joining the Society) who had arrived at the Cape in 1817 to begin his work among the Nama of the western seaboard. He took over the Lattakoo mission in 1821, pursuaded the chief to move his headquarters closer to the source of the Kuruman River and, initially, devoted much of his time to building

a new station (henceforth referred to as Kuruman). He had all the qualities the job demanded – moral rectitude, a passion for discipline, an enormous capacity for hard work, the ability to organize, a

An elegant two-some of the Tlhaping group. These people were the first to receive Christian missionaries.

Robert Moffat: friend both to the Tswana and Mzilikazi's Ndebele.

laudable determination to learn the language and ways of his Tswana hosts, and an all-consuming religious zeal. But he, like those before him, failed to make any real headway in the early years: it wasn't until 1829 that he could claim his first Christian convert.

Many of the troubles that beset Moffat's ministry during the first decade, though, were of alien origin and quite beyond his power to influence. For the greater part of Southern Africa, that which lay beyond the narrow confines of European occupation, this was a violent and confused period, characterized by what is known as the *difaqane*.

The turbulent years

To digress a little from the main story, the *difaqane*, in its simplest definition, was the forced migration of millions of tribesmen, initially triggered by the slave and ivory trades in the Delagoa Bay – modern Maputo – area of Mozambique, a flashpoint reinforced by British military operations on the far-off eastern Cape 'frontier'. Both slave-raiders and army deliberately destroyed the assets of the local communities, reducing thousands to the status of refugees. The upheaval ignited a chain reaction of violence and counter-

violence as the uprooted tribes encroached on and fought for neighbouring lands, the defeated group moving on to displace others who, in their turn, migrated to spread fire, sword and famine in the farther reaches. The *difaqane*, in short, represented the domino principle in classic and devastating action.

Part of this migratory wave washed over what was to become Bechuanaland and, later, Botswana. Among the immigrants – part refugees, part marauders – was a Tlokwa group led by the firebrand chieftainess MaNtatisi and her son Sekonyela. Even more formidable was a section of the Bakololo people who, under the leadership of Sebetwane, set out on a fighting march from the Orange River and across the Kalahari to found the Makololo (or Kololo) kingdom of the middle Zambezi.

These were dramatic and at times dangerous years for the missionaries of Kuruman. The most eventful, perhaps, was 1823, which saw an aggressive horde of Hlakwana and Phuting in occupation of the old capital of Dithakong and intent on doing battle with the local Tlhaping. After an unsuccessful attempt at peace-keeping, Moffat rode south to enlist the help of the mixed-descent Griqua, and brought a hundred or so of

their mounted riflemen back with him to rout the invaders – and, incidentally, to take about a hundred slaves, which he sold in the northern Cape.

One of the most noteworthy of the *difaqane*'s 'ripples' to reach the broader region – certainly in the context of European involvement in its affairs – was the arrival of Mzilikazi, a brilliant Zulu general who had quarrelled with Shaka and fled northwards with 300 Kumalo warriors. His 'raiding kingdom', now known as the Ndebele, moved first north and then westwards, defeating and absorbing the local Sotho peoples until it reached the Magaliesberg hills, finally turning north again to settle around the Marico River, close to modern Botswana's south-eastern border.

Once entrenched in the area, Mzilikazi tolerated and even welcomed European travellers and churchmen, and was especially taken with Robert Moffat who, though the two men met on only five occasions, exerted an extraordinary influence over the Ndebele king: Mzilikazi, the scourge of the local Tswana people, never converted to Christianity but he did listen carefully to and sometimes acted upon Moffat's advice, both moral and practical.

Other white men, though, were less diplomatic and, in physical terms, a lot

Lattakoo, site of the London Missionary Society's first station, from a sketch by the celebrated William Burchell.

more powerful. In the mid-1830s thousands of Boer families, disenchanted with the British colonial administration in Cape Town, had inspanned their oxen and trekked into the interior in search of solitude and the right to govern themselves. Their vanguard crossed the Orange and then the Vaal River and, in 1836, probed into the Ndebele lands, threatening Mzilikazi's territorial authority. In that year, after annihilating some isolated Boer parties, Ndebele impis advanced against the main body of trekkers, but were decisively defeated at Vegkop and, later, at Mosega (the Ndebele capital, target of a dawn raid which was more of a massacre than a battle) and Kapain (alternatively known as Engabeni). Numbers and raw courage had proved no match for the devastating firepower of the newcomers and Mzilikazi, acknowledging the realities, led his people north yet again, across the Limpopo River to the Bulawayo region of today's Zimbabwe. Here he re-created the Ndebele state in a network of regimental villages that proved strong enough to resist further encroachment by Boer parties.

Tswana and Boer

By this time, the London Missionary Society (LMS) had established a white presence well to the north of Kuruman – among the Bakwena, the Bangwato and the Bangwaketsi in today's eastern Botswana, and even among the Tswana in the remoteness of Ngamiland in the north-central region. And as the missionaries widened their pastoral horizons so did their influence grow – not, let it be said, because the Tswana were particularly avid to hear The Word, but rather for the knowledge and worldly sophistication the clerics brought with them. These were changing times; outside elements were beginning to take a competitive interest in the region and the old Tswana ways, long protected by isolation, were being threatened. Understandably, the chiefs turned to the kindliest and least dangerous of the intruders, those who came simply to preach the Christian Gospel, for guidance in dealing with the new complexities that faced them.

Their most immediate concern was the Voortrekker encroachment from the south. Admittedly the Boers had rescued them from the depredations of Mzilikazi, but white occupation of the region that was soon to become the Transvaal Republic posed its own dangers. There were disputes over land rights and the occasional outbreak of open conflict, notably between the newcomers to the region and the Kwena section of the Tswana.

The Boers were nervous of the powerful, independent chiefdoms that fringed their settlements in the north-east. They were also deeply distrustful of the English-speaking hunters, traders and, especially, the missionaries who had ingratiated themselves with the Tswana and who formed an increasingly effective barrier to the new territory's northward expansion. Their particular *bête noir* was David Livingstone, the great missionary-explorer, who had married Robert Moffat's daughter Mary and, in 1845, ensconced himself among the Kwena.

Livingstone had converted Kwena

David Livingstone, counsellor to the Kwena people, fiercely opposed Boer ambitions.

chief Sechele to Christianity and, according to rumour (probably unfounded), was helping the Kwena to obtain firearms. However that may be, the LMS certainly supported the Tswana in their resistance to Boer territorial ambitions and the Boers, for their part, were determined to secure and extend their frontiers. In 1852, Sechele's capital of Dimawe was raided and the nearby mission station ransacked – the most dramatic of a succession of incidents that soured Boer–Tswana relations in the mid-19th century. (The Boers did not emerge unscathed: they lost 20 or so men in the raid, and the Bakwena then pursued them, burning some of their farms, forcing them into laager and then out of the Zeerust area altogether.) Livingstone wasn't present when this happened – other, remoter regions beckoned; he had already explored Lake Ngami and parts of the Zambezi valley and he would shortly embark on the first of his epic journeys. He did, though, roundly condemn the Dimawe violation and made his views known, forcefully, to the British government.

Central to these conflicts was the so-called 'Missionaries' Road', the route that ran up through the eastern part of the Tswana territory and which provided the only practical means of access to the northern interior. The Boers recognized its strategic value, and claimed as their western boundary an area that embraced both the road and the Tswana lands that straddled it.

All this caused barely a ripple on the comparatively placid surface of international politics at the time. The frenetic 'scramble for Africa' had not yet started, and the British colonial authorities, rather than risk an expensive and profitless confrontation, preferred to reach a cosy understanding with the Boers. At the Sand River Convention of 1852, which conferred virtual independence on the Transvaal, it was agreed that the 'immigrant farmers' would control the territory north of the Vaal more or less without let or hindrance provided they kept to their own side of the river. The British also promised not to enter into alliances with the Tswana and other indigenous peoples to the north.

Polishing diamonds at the Teemane diamond centre at Serowe village. Botswana today ranks as a world leader in diamond production.

Gold, diamonds and disputes

For a time the Tswana were left in relative peace. What regional aspirations the Boers had were confined to southern Bechuanaland, and even these were inhibited by bitter rivalries within the Transvaal, and by its leader's preoccupation with unity (at one point, in 1859, M.W. Pretorius found himself president of the Orange Free State as well as of his own country). But by 1860 the dust had settled: internal political differences were patched up, Pretoria became the new Transvaal capital, and the Boers were able to turn their attention once again to their western boundary.

The region to their west, indeed, was now beginning to provoke serious colonial competition. In 1867 gold was discovered around the Dati River, a disputed territory claimed by both the Ndebele of the north and by the Ngwato group of the Tswana. A year later Transvaal's President Pretorius made his move, bidding not only for the goldfields but for the whole of the Missionaries' Road. Yet his annexation of the vast area – most of what constituted Bechuanaland at the time – still failed to provoke the British. Despite the Ngwato chief Matseng's plea for intervention, Britain declined to take over the goldfields and their unruly diggers (they did,

though, withhold recognition of the annexation).

The situation during the next few years remained confused, at times downright chaotic.

In 1868 diamonds were discovered around the confluence of the Vaal and Harts rivers to the south and, a year later, in massive quantities in the Kimberley area of Griqualand West, prompting a flurry of claims and counter-claims involving the Transvaal and Orange Free State republics, the Cape Colony, the mixed-descent Griquas and the southern Tswana groups.

In due course Griqualand West was transferred to the Cape Colony (by the Keate Award of 1871) and the boundary between the Tswana (notably the Barolong) and the Transvaal defined – but unconvincingly so, and the Boers continued to encroach westwards. In 1878, following general unrest in the region and an attempt at open rebellion by elements of the Tswana, a small force of colonial police occupied southern Bechuanaland. When this was withdrawn in 1881, the region lapsed into anarchy.

And the Boers renewed their westward push, even though the Pretoria Convention of that year formally established, for the first time, the borders of the Transvaal on all sides.

Competing forces

In the early 1880s a section of the Barolong to the south of the Molopo River, beset by factional quarrels, invited freebooters from the western Transvaal to settle on Tswana territory, offering them land and cattle in return for 'protective services' against their local enemies – a move which led to the creation of two Boer mini-republics, which the freebooters named Stellaland and Goshen.

The government in Pretoria, although resisting the temptation to take over the two territories immediately, again pressed for an extension of the Transvaal's western borders, and remained confident that at some point in the not distant future, amid all the confusion, they would be able to mount a successful land grab.

The threat caused deep concern to two powerful bodies of political interest:

The British imperialists Both the politicians and the public in Britain, hitherto somewhat insular in outlook, had shed their apathy and, their imaginations fed by chauvinistic international rivalries, were now taking a keen interest in events in far-off Africa. The Germans had established a tentative presence on the south-western seaboard (the region now named Namibia), were edging inland and could soon, it was believed, cross the Kalahari in the east to link up with the Transvaal Boers – a junction that would effectively block the Missionaries' Road, and everyone else's aspirations, to the northern interior.

Moreover, a number of humanitarians – notably John Mackenzie, a passionate defender of African rights and successor to Moffat at Kuruman – were campaigning vigorously for direct British involvement in Bechuanaland, lending moral force to an otherwise cynically political policy that sought to contain the Boers.

The British Cape Cecil Rhodes, leader of the opposition in the Cape colonial parliament and an increasingly influential force in Southern African affairs, also regarded the Boers with deep suspicion. He and his political cronies in

Cape Town – men who shared his grand (some would say megalomaniac) visions of empire – viewed the Kalahari region generally and the Missionaries' Road in particular as the Suez Canal of Africa, the Imperial way across the Limpopo and into the vast territory of what is now Zimbabwe.

In 1883 President Paul Kruger of the Transvaal led a delegation to Britain to seek revision of the Pretoria Convention, but found the government in cautious mood: the London Convention of the following year contained only minor adjustments to the western border. Of more significance was the declaration of a British protectorate over 'the country outside the Transvaal' – a vague phrase taken to mean the territory south of the Molopo River.

Britain's new protective policy, though, was more honoured in its definition than its execution. First Mackenzie and then, rather improbably, Rhodes himself was recruited to bring some order to the troubled territory. Neither succeeded in making headway. Rhodes's administration was bedevilled especially by the wild republicans of Goshen, who attacked the Barolong at Mafeking.

Cecil Rhodes, the `immense and brooding spirit', planned to colonize Bechuanaland. His scheme failed after representations by Tswana chiefs and white missionaries.

Shortly afterwards Paul Kruger sent in a commando to annex the Barolong lands, and for a brief period Transvaal's *Vierkleur* flag flew over the town, enabling Boer farmers to carve up the surrounding countryside.

The British finally lost their patience, sending Sir Charles Warren in with a small army to pacify the region (which he did without firing a shot in anger) and, in 1885, formally extending the protectorate northward. The region south of the Molopo River was designated the Crown Colony of Bechuanaland (or British Bechuanaland for short) which, ten years later and principally at Rhodes's instigation, became part of the Cape Colony. The regions to the north, now constituted as the Bechuanaland Protectorate, were progressively enlarged over the next few years to embrace the areas up to the Shashe River, the Tati district, and later the vast Ngwato chiefdom, ruled by the enlightened Khama III, and the plains that lay to the north and west – in short, modern Botswana more or less in its entirety.

In time, after Warren was withdrawn, Sir Sidney Shippard was appointed administrator of the colony and deputy commissioner for the protectorate.

Rhodes and Khama

During the early 1890s Bechuanaland played a central role in Cecil Rhodes's scheme to colonize the whole of south-central Africa – the first stage of a grand design that envisaged no less than a British Africa eventually stretching from Cape Town to Cairo.

His Pioneer Column, armed vanguard of the chartered British South Africa (BSA) Company, mustered at Macloutsie (Motloutse) before embarking on its final push through Matabeleland and on to Fort Salisbury (which it occupied in September 1890). Thereafter the first Rhodesians depended on the supply routes through the protectorate; and it was through Bechuanaland that the first railway from the Cape later snaked its way northwards.

Not surprisingly, therefore, Bechuanaland figured prominently in Rhodes's wider territorial scheme and in the mid-1990s, armed with his wide-ranging

Royal Charter, he almost persuaded the British government to transfer authority over the protectorate to his BSA Company. His plot, however, failed: ranged against him were, among others, the London Missionary Society and a number of influential Tswana leaders, most notably Khama III, paramount chief of the Ngwato.

Khama, who had converted to Christianity in 1862 and succeeded to the paramountcy a decade later, was a man of ability, steadfast character and unusual courage. As a senior prince of the royal family he had successfully defended his people against Ndebele marauders from the north and his faith against a father who held passionately to the traditional Tswana ways (Khama refused either to attend the Tswana tribal school or to take a second wife – decisions which at one point almost cost him his life). Now, formally entrenched in chiefly office and universally respected for his wisdom, he led a delegation to London and extracted from the colonial secretary, Joseph Chamberlain, an assurance that his country would remain under the Crown's protection. In return, the Tswana leaders agreed to cede to the BSA Company strips of land in the eastern region for the construction of the railway to Rhodesia.

Rhodes's immediate plans had been successfully frustrated, and any further designs he may have harboured on the protectorate faded with the abortive Jameson Raid of 1895/6 (his Rhodesian raiders, who intended taking Johannesburg by force of arms, had used Bechuanaland as a springboard).

Towards independence

In 1895 the Colony of British Bechuanaland – the territory lying to the south of the Molopo River – was transferred to the Cape which in turn, fifteen years later, became one of the four provinces of the Union of South Africa. The Bechuanaland Protectorate to the north, on the other hand, remained a British dependency until it gained full autonomy in 1966. Up to 1961 the territory was administered by a Resident Commissioner under the direction of the British High

Commissioner in South Africa, who was also responsible for the kingdoms of Swaziland and Basutoland (Lesotho) which were now independent. Curiously, the protectorate's administrative headquarters, or capital, remained at Mafeking (modern Mafikeng), which lay outside its borders.

The first few decades of the century passed in unremarkable fashion: there was practically no political development and, in consequence, very little progress was made on the economic and social fronts. Life went on virtually undisturbed by change of any kind, the routines regulated by a colonial power made lethargic by Bechuanaland's remoteness, its apparent poverty and lack of strategic importance. To London, the territory was a backwater, a drain on the exchequer that merited little attention and even less financial outlay. This indifference was compounded by a vague assumption that the three High Commission protectorates would in due course be absorbed by the Union of South Africa (indeed, there was reference to just such an eventuality in the South Africa Act of 1909).

In the event, the issue became the subject of some controversy. On several occasions South Africa pressed for incorporation, but the British had become increasingly cautious in its dealings with a dominion that, almost before the ink had dried on the unifying Act, had begun to legislate away the rights of its black citizens. The British government made its position clear on 20 June 1935: there would be no transfer of authority until the inhabitants of Bechuanaland had been consulted, and until the House of Commons had debated the question. These principles were formally confirmed several times in later years.

Among the most newsworthy events of the pre-independence period was the 1948 marriage of Seretse (later Sir Seretse) Khama, grandson of Khama III and heir to the Ngwato paramount chieftaincy, to Ruth Williams, an Englishwoman. The union was hotly debated in political and press circles and became something of an international *cause célèbre*, for the British government not only refused to recognize Seretse's right

A display of family photographs in the Khama III Memorial Museum, Serowe, highlights the enormous pressures placed upon Seretse Khama and his English wife, Ruth, in the early years of their marriage.

to royal succession should he marry a white woman, but banished him from the country of his birth. The decisions were prompted by influential elements among the traditional Ngwato, who found it difficult to accept a white commoner as a member of their royal family. South Africa, which declared Seretse a 'prohibited immigrant', had also brought pressure to bear.

Seretse's father, Sekgoma II, died when Seretse was just four years old and he grew up under his uncle Tshekedi's regency, later attending Lovedale, Fort Hare and Witwatersrand (Johannesburg) universities, where he read for a law degree. In 1945 he travelled to England to continue his studies at Oxford and London's Inner Temple, and it was during these student years that he met his future wife. At first he declined to renounce the chieftainship (the British government had, rather tactlessly,

offered him an annual stipend of £1 100 to do so) but in 1956, in exchange for permission to return to his native country, he reversed his decision. For some years he and Ruth lived quietly in Bechuanaland, without the trappings of high office but contributing a lot to the community – and gaining the deep respect of the people.

British Prime Minister Harold Macmillan's momentous 'winds of change' address to a joint sitting of the South African parliament in 1960 heralded profound changes within the southern subcontinent. His message was plain: Britain's future lay in Europe, and her colonies would henceforth have to fend for themselves. A year later South Africa precipitously departed from the Commonwealth. For the High Commission territories, surrounded as they now were by a powerful and potentially hostile Republic, independence had become an urgent priority.

At the end of 1960 Bechuanaland received a new constitution comprising an Executive Council, a Legislative Council (one with an unoffical majority) and an advisory African Council created principally to elect the African members of the legislative body. The dispensation was temporary, designed to prepare the way for an independence constitution, the framework for which was agreed by representatives of all the parties in 1963 and implemented in 1965. At the general election in March of that year the newly knighted Sir Seretse Khama's Bechuanaland Democratic Party (BDP) won 28 of the 31 parliamentary seats to become premier of a self-governing Bechuanaland. The territory's capital was moved from Mafeking to Gaborone (then spelt Gaberones).

The country formally received its independence, as Botswana, on 30 September 1966 when Princess Marina, the Duchess of Kent, representing Queen Elizabeth, handed over the reins of power in Gaborone's national assembly building before a distinguished gathering of international representatives. The subsequent celebrations were dignified, even muted, devoid of the hysteria that had accompanied the granting of freedom in many other parts of Africa.

The free country

In terms of the constitution Sir Seretse Khama became Botswana's first executive president, to remain as head of state until his death in July 1980. He was succeeded by Dr Quett Masire, vice-president and co-founder of the Bechuanaland (later Botswana) Democratic Party (BDP) which, pursuing pragmatic policies based on non-racialism, a mixed economy and respect for democratic rights, has enjoyed an overwhelming parliamentary majority during the nearly three decades since the granting of independence.

The BDP has succeeded in sustaining economic growth (which has been impressive by any standards, especially since the first of the diamond mines came on stream in 1971) and this, together with often desperately needed drought relief measures, has guaranteed

it the support of the rural population. The BDP's chief rival has been the Botswana National Front, a socialist party that favours land reform (to narrow the income gap between rich and poor in the countryside) and accelerated industrialization (to meet the growing demand for jobs). The BDP has consistently drawn three-quarters of the popular vote, the BNF between 15 and 20 per cent, and five other, smaller parties the remainder.

The newly independent country's entry into the regional political arena brought its predictable share of problems. John Vorster, South Africa's premier in the late 1960s, had lifted the prohibition on Sir Seretse Khama, stating that Botswana's independence was in accord with the apartheid regime's own 'homelands' policy. He furthermore suggested that Botswana should become a member of a proposed Southern African federation.

This Sir Seretse dismissed with contempt. Botswana, he said, wasn't prepared to become a 'bantustan' and, in any case, such a move would cut across the country's ties with black Africa and inhibit its function as a bridge between north and south.

Botswana's government, in fact, faced something of a dilemma: on the one hand it administered a poor and landlocked region entirely dependent on the communications network and economic wealth of a southern neighbour despised for its racial policies while, on the other, it had a natural affinity with and was drawn towards the liberated nations of the continent, who were united in their condemnation of South Africa. Somehow, Botswana had to maintain a delicate balance between the two. The rebellion of Ian Smith's white hardliners in next-door Rhodesia, in November 1965, had further complicated matters.

That Botswana managed to survive and even prosper within these constrictions is a tribute to the common sense and moderation of its leadership. Not that the path through the maze of conflicting pressures was trouble free. On the contrary, the country was caught up in the Rhodesian imbroglio during the 1970s (it became a haven for refugees

from the civil war, and for Joshua Nkomo's Zipra guerilla forces) and relations with South Africa remained tense for two decades.

Between 1984 and 1986 Pretoria, worried by the infiltration of African National Congress (ANC) guerillas, pressed for a mutual security pact, a proposal which President Masire dismissed out of hand, though he did confirm that Botswana would not be used as a launching pad for attacks against its southern neighbour. Nevertheless the liberation struggle spilled over the borders: in 1985 there were bomb blasts aimed at South African refugees and a commando raid against ANC 'military' targets in Gaborone (in which eleven people, some of them Botswana nationals, were killed), followed by other violations, a number perpetrated by South African undercover agents. The Botswana government, recognizing the country's vulnerability, took action against 'illegal immigrants', asked the ANC representative to withdraw, and sponsored a National Security Act that provided for arrest without warrant and long terms of imprisonment for 'acts of terrorism and sabotage'. South Africa, however, continued its harassment, the most serious of its incursions a commando-style raid on a 'terrorist' house in Gaborone in March 1988.

But within two years the situation had undergone a spectacular transformation. Internal instability, international pressure and the end of the Cold War between the superpowers introduced new and kindlier elements onto the Southern African political scene. Early in 1990 South Africa's president, F.W. de Klerk, unbanned the African National Congress and other liberation organizations, released a large number of political prisoners (including the ANC's Nelson Mandela, who had lived behind bars for the past 27 years) and put his country firmly on the long, hard road to full democracy.

The tensions lifted immediately. Botswana and its neighbours, for the first time in decades, could now look forward to peaceful development within a wider region no longer threatened by racial antagonisms.

BOTSWANA TODAY

Botswana is often cited as a model for the rest of the African continent, and with good reason: it's a well-run country, stable, prosperous, and uncompromisingly democratic. Like every developing country, it has its problems, but these are relatively minor, some of them ironically stemming from an embarrassment of riches (the huge diamond mines) and from the income disparities that these accentuate, then from the lack of resources, over-population and grinding poverty that afflict so much of Africa.

Government

At independence in 1966 Botswana adopted the Westminster constitutional system. Legislative authority was vested in a National Assembly then comprising 34 members elected by universal adult suffrage, four nominated members, the Speaker and the attorney-general (who does not have a parliamentary vote). The president, who is elected for a period corresponding to the life of the National Assembly (and may be re-elected for further terms) is both head of state and executive head of government, presiding over a cabinet drawn from the Assembly. The president is also a parliamentarian, speaking on matters affecting his own portfolios (external affairs, internal security, defence, the civil service).

The once all-powerful hereditary chiefs no longer play a pre-eminent role in national politics: tribalism remains strongly entrenched in the rural areas, but it runs counter to government's declared non-racial policies and indeed to the spirit of the constitution and, with urbanization and the loosening of feudal ties, is in decline. There is, however, a House of Chiefs that advises the government on tribal matters, and no laws affecting traditional rights and customs, nor amendments to the constitution, may be passed without reference to it. The House consists of the chiefs of the eight principal Tswana groups (see page 11), who have permanent seats, together with seven lesser elected members. Entrenched in the constitution is a code of human rights whose provisions are enforceable by the High Court.

The Seretse Khama Memorial fronts the National Assembly in Gaborone, the country's capital.

Justice

The High Court, comprising the chief justice and associate (or puisne) judges, has jurisdiction in civil and criminal cases; matters emanating from it are heard in the Court of Appeal. Subordinate courts and African courts have limited jurisdiction in the country's dozen administrative districts. Hereditary chiefs still exercise authority in issues of custom and traditional usage, and in regulating village affairs – though not in the allocation of land.

Foreign affairs and security

Botswana is a member of the Organisation of African Unity (OAU) and has played an active part both in the Southern African Development Co-ordinating Conference (SADCC, a body which has sought to minimize regional economic dependence on South Africa), and in a loose grouping known as the Frontline States.

Events, however – the abandonment of apartheid and South Africa's reacceptance into the community of nations –

have overtaken the latter two organizations, though the SADCC will have an important new role to play, perhaps with South African participation. The political climate in Southern Africa favours new associations and collective initiatives although, at the time of writing, no clear pattern had emerged. Nevertheless, Botswana is likely to adopt a positive approach to co-operative ventures in the fields of communications, trade (the country has long been a member of the Southern African Customs Union that also embraces South Africa, Namibia, Lesotho and Swaziland), energy, conservation and tourism.

During the first decade of independence Botswana had no standing army – the police, and in particular its respected mobile unit, handled both internal and border security. In 1977, however, the unstable situation created by Rhodesia's escalating bush war and the low-intensity conflict between ANC infiltrators and the South African security establishment prompted the formation of a well-trained permanent force of 4 500 men. In the early 1990s the Botswana Defence Force (BDF) comprised five infantry battalions, one armoured battalion, a squadron of combat aircraft and a number of military helicopters. The 1989/90 Budget allocation for defence exceeded the previous year's by 57 per cent, although since then of course regional tensions have decreased and, in theory, there is now far less need for a strong military capability.

Education

Since independence, progress in this sphere has been remarkable: education absorbs a quarter of the national budgeted revenue; children enter school at the age of six and tuition for the country's 300 000-plus primary pupils is free. Seven out of ten go on to secondary schools (a major secondary expansion programme is under way), which currently have a combined enrolment of around 50 000.

Higher education is provided by the University of Botswana in Gaborone and at several teacher-training colleges; more than 10 000 students receive technical training at the 70 or so vocational centres – a field that is receiving high priority in a national effort to reduce the shortage of skilled workers in an increasingly urbanized society.

Health

Among the more prevalent diseases in Botswana are gastro-enteritis; illnesses related to malnutrition (which reaches serious proportions during the periodic droughts: in 1985 the World Food Programme calculated that more than a third of the population was 'vulnerable' to malnourishment); malaria (principally in and around the Chobe area, Ngamiland and northern wetland region); the human immuno-deficiency virus (HIV, leading to AIDS) and its sinister bedfellow, tuberculosis.

However, health services are well above average Third World standards, reaching an impressive 90 per cent of the population which, as we've noted, is concentrated in the eastern region. Among these services are 15 general hospitals, a dozen health-care centres and a great many clinics and health posts. In the early 1990s, life expectancy stood at around 60 years.

Housing

An acute shortage of serviced stands (droughts have led to moratoriums on water connections) has impeded the provision of low-cost housing – which, in the context of a spectacular growth in urban population, creates serious socioeconomic problems. However, development is being accelerated; the Botswana Housing Corporation, for instance, is building 14 000 units in Gaborone alone, despite a rapid escalation of construction costs.

At the time of independence in 1966 Botswana (previously the Bechuanaland Protectorate) had no capital city as such and it was decided that Gaborone, then a sleepy village of about 6 000 inhabitants, would have to suffice. Today it is a thriving city of more than 145 000 people and one of the fastest growing on the African continent.

ECONOMIC POINTERS

Botswana is one of Africa's richest countries – indeed, the World Bank ranks it the world's leading performer in terms of per capita Gross Domestic Product growth (GDP per capita rose from 40 pula at independence in 1966 to 4 900 pula in 1990) and per capita income growth (4,5 per cent a year since independence), outstripping even the 'miracle economies' of the Pacific Rim. The economy, classed as 'mixed' (market forces are allowed fairly free play but there is state intervention in key areas), is well managed and buoyant, recording an average annual growth rate of 11 per cent during the 1980s. A series of national plans since 1967 has given priority to energy needs, mining, the beef industry, and crop production. The seventh plan was launched in 1991.

The economy, however, remains unbalanced: the country's wellbeing is almost entirely dependent on cattle and diamonds, which are vulnerable, respectively, to drought and the vagaries of the world market for precious stones. Botswana is also over-reliant on South Africa for food, manufactured goods and transport – a situation that happily carries a lot less risk in the more amiable political climate that has prevailed since the demise of the apartheid regime.

At independence, the national wealth was derived almost exclusively from large-scale ranching, and Botswana needed international donor aid to finance development, but the discovery and exploitation of diamond resources and, later, of rich copper-nickel deposits has transformed the economy. Mining has replaced cattle as the principal money-spinner, and the revenue from diamond exports has enabled the government not only to pay its way but to embark on ambitious road-building and other infrastructural projects. The social sectors, notably education and health, have also derived enormous benefit from the diamond boom.

Nevertheless, more than 75 per cent of the people still depend in one way or another on livestock, the great majority of them at subsistence level; agricultural

Cattle rancher and Maun businessman David Kays and his son Martin oversee a portion of their beef herd in the Haneveld region of the central Kalahari district.

wealth – the herds, and income from the meat-processing industry – remains in the hands of the few. This, together with frequent droughts, has given impetus to the migration of rural families to the towns, and the consequent unemployment has created serious social problems. In short, the economic upswing has rewarded the cattle baron and the urban wage-earner, leaving the majority almost as badly off as they were in the pre-diamond era. Correcting this imbalance is probably the toughest of the challenges facing government planners.

However, from the general to the particular:

Agriculture

This sector's share of the Gross Domestic Product declined dramatically during the 1980s, plunging from 16 per cent (in the 1978/9 year) to just 3 per cent (1987/8) but, as we have mentioned, the land still provides a living for great numbers of people and thus remains one of the twin pillars of the economy.

Climate and soils favour large-scale ranching; the national cattle herd numbers between two and three million depending on rainfall (around a million head died during the great drought that lasted from 1983 to 1987). One twenti-

eth of the country's 50 000 ranchers own more than half the cattle; one in two rural households own no cattle at all. Many country families, though, keep sheep and goats. The number of small stock, which is generally better able to withstand drought conditions, hovers around the two-million mark.

The authorities are investing a lot of time and money in the improvement of ranching techniques and in land tenure reform in an effort to stabilize production and limit over-grazing. Prime ingredient of the latter programme is the fencing of leasehold properties – an expensive, difficult and, in terms of wildlife conservation, controversial process (see pages 50 and 51).

The processing of beef, which accounts for 80 per cent of agricultural production, is undertaken by the monopoly Botswana Meat Commission (BMC) in its abattoirs in Lobatse (Africa's largest), Maun and Francistown. Over 95 per cent of the output is exported, mainly to South Africa, the United Kingdom and the European Economic Community, to which preferential access is enjoyed through the provisions of the Lome Conventions. The BMC also runs a 4 000-tonne capacity cold store in London and a corned-beef canning plant in Botswana.

Despite strenuous efforts to promote self-sufficiency, crop production – notably of maize, millet, beans and, especially, sorghum – remains at a disappointingly low level, accounting for less than a third of agricultural output even in years of good rainfall. The country, as we've noted, imports most of its food needs from South Africa. Various irrigation schemes – which will tap the Limpopo, Shashe, Lotsane and other rivers – promise much, though a similar onslaught on the waters of the western Okavango Delta has drawn fierce opposition from both the local tourist industry and environmentalists throughout the world.

Fishing, mainly in the northern river-valley and Okavango regions, provides a valuable additional food source. Forestry also contributes its share: the perennial need for firewood has played havoc with Botswana's natural forests but the teak, mukwa, mahogany and other hardwoods of the Chobe area hold promise for the timber industry (Kasane has a sawmill) and eucalyptus, or gumtree, plantations have been established around Serowe, Mochudi and Molepolele.

Mining

The mining sector is the powerhouse of Botswana's thriving economy, its contribution accounting for around two-fifths of the Gross Domestic Product and 90 per cent of the country's total export earnings.

Large-scale mineral production began in 1971, when the De Beers Botswana Mining Company (Debswana), in which the government has a substantial interest, started working the rich diamond 'pipe' at Orapa, in the bleak Kalahari countryside south of the Makgadikgadi pans. Other mines followed: the smaller Letlhakane, close to Orapa, in 1977 and the exciting Jwaneng enterprise, near Kanye in the south-eastern region, in 1982. Combined output totals some 15 million carats a year, which is marketed on an exclusive basis by the De Beers' Central Selling Organisation (CSO; the contract will be reviewed in 1995). Jwaneng has proved especially rewarding (see page 19).

The copper-nickel industry, concentrated around Selebi-Phikwe in the east, had a less auspicious beginning – the huge Shashe Project (which embraces water and power undertakings as well as mining), was plagued by technical and debt problems in the decade after its inauguration in 1974. Towards the end of the 1980s, however, metal prices improved somewhat, production began (in 1989) at the Selkirk deposit east of Francistown, a new shaft (Selebi North) came on stream in 1991, and the industry is now playing an increasingly important role in the country's economy. The Tati Nickel Mining Company, which has an interest in the Selkirk venture, also owns the rights to the nearby and very promising Phoenix orebody.

After a 20-year gestation period the vast Sowa Pan brine deposits in the Makgadikgadi area began yielding soda-ash and salt. The project, managed by South Africa's African Explosives and Chemical Industries (AECI) conglomerate – though Anglo American, De Beers and the Botswana government also hold shares – employs about 500 people and has prompted much-needed regional investment in roads, a rail link, water supplies and other infrastructure. Annual production targets have been pegged at 650 000 tonnes of salt and 300 000

tonnes of soda-ash, technically known as sodium carbonate and used in the manufacture of glass, chemicals (caustic soda, baking soda, washing soda), pulp, paper, soap and other detergents, and in the metallurgical and petroleum industries. The targets have not yet been achieved, but nevertheless Botswana has replaced the United States as South Africa's principal supplier of the product.

Other riches lie beneath the ground, some of them in as yet undetermined quantities: aerial surveys have revealed promising orebodies of the platinum group of metals, chromium, asbestos and manganese. Coal is mined by the Morupule Colliery (a subsidiary of the Anglo American Corporation) near Palapye to supply the Selebi-Phikwe copper-nickel workings and the town's thermal station. Eastern Botswana's coal reserves have been estimated at a massive 17 billion tonnes, but the depressed world market for the commodity has inhibited large-scale development. Small quantities of gold are mined in the Francistown area. The quarrying industry has been galvanized by demand for crushed stone from a booming construction sector. Manufacturing and construction together account for around 10 per cent of the Gross Domestic Product.

The huge open-cast Jwaneng diamond mine is ranked among the world's richest: it produces 9 million carats a year, a third of which are of gem quality.

Secondary industry

Most of the country's manufacturing enterprises are associated with and dependent on the mining and agricultural sectors, but serious efforts are being made – notably by the Botswana Development Corporation (BDC) – to diversify. Political tranquillity, a strategic geographical position, favourable exchange control regulations and general economic prosperity are proving attractive to investors despite a shortage of skills, expensive land and housing and the smallness of the local market, and there has been impressive progress. At the beginning of the 1990s the BDC either owned or had a substantial stake in about a hundred ventures, including two breweries, an iron foundry, and concrete, milling and sugar-packing enterprises as well as hotel, estate management and insurance services. Among multinationals that have a stake in Botswana are Lonrho (textiles) and Colgate-Palmolive (soaps, detergents, cosmetics). A valuable portion of new overseas investment drawn to the subcontinent following South Africa's emergence from isolation has been channelled into Botswana, preferred to its more economically advanced southern neighbour for its social stability. Typical is the multimillion dollar Owens-Corning glass-reinforced plastic pipe factory projected for Gaborone.

Labour and prices

Unemployment is a serious problem: the formal sector can provide work for barely 20 per cent of the economically active population. In the latter part of the 1980s just on 180 000 people had permanent jobs (28 per cent of them in the public service) and it was reckoned that 21 000 work-seekers were coming onto the market each year.

Government policy is based on the assumption that money spent on job creation is money largely wasted. It seeks instead to do everything possible to provide more opportunities in the 'informal sector' and the rural areas, and to encourage employers to expand their workforces through wage restraints and other incentives. This two-pronged

A modern telecommunications tower rises above the traditional mud huts of Mopipi, a typical Botswana village in a remote corner of the Kalahari.

approach has already borne fruit.

Strikes are relatively rare occurrences in Botswana (though teachers and bank employees downed their pens in 1989). Trade unions – there are about 20 of them – bargain with employers through a system of wage councils. The cost of living (and therefore wages) is largely determined by price movements in South Africa, which supplies most of Botswana's food and manufactured goods. Inflation has been running at an annual rate of about 15 per cent.

Infrastructure

Botswana's sound financial position and excellent prospects have enabled its government to invest heavily in the twin pillars of a sound economy – energy and communications.

Energy

The Botswana Power Corporation (BPC) meets the country's electricity needs, mainly through its coal-fired thermal stations, though a small amount of electricity is supplied by South Africa's giant Eskom utility.

Botswana imports its fuel requirements, but the country could become

self-sufficient in the not-too-distant future: there may be viable deposits of oils and natural gas locked away beneath the Kgalagadi basin in the west and the Ncojane basins of the northwest. Exploration continues, notably by the Petro-Canada Corporation.

Roads

The national network comprises a little over 8 000 kilometres of roads, of which 1 500 kilometres are fully tarred. Well-maintained highways connect Gaborone and Francistown with the main tourist areas – Maun (for the Okavango Delta and Moremi Game Reserve) and Kasane (for the Chobe park and, with the completion of the proposed road bridge over the Zambezi, for Livingstone and the Victoria Falls). The main east-west route also provides access to the Makgadikgadi pans and to more distant destinations: it now extends beyond Maun to Shakawe and Namibia's Caprivi region.

In 1990 Botswana and Namibia reached concensus on the construction of a trans-Kalahari highway linking Gaborone with Windhoek, and work on the first 80-kilometre stretch of the

Botswana portion started shortly after the agreement was signed.

These, though, are the trunk roads. For the rest, movement around this immense and largely empty country can be a difficult and frustrating business for the independent motorist bent on exploring the wilder spaces: distances are enormous; the roads long, lonely, often rough and devoid of signposts. Travellers need a four-wheel-drive vehicle to get around parts of the Moremi reserve, the Okavango swamplands, the Chobe park and the Makgadikgadi area; journeys through the central and southern Kalahari wilderness can – unless one is careful to stock up with motor spares, extra fuel, water, plenty of provisions and a good map – involve real risk.

Railways

Practically all the country's rail traffic – 1 400 million ton-km of freight and half a million passengers a year – is carried along the 900-kilometre line that leads from Ramatlabama on the South African border, north through Lobatse, Gaborone and Francistown to Plumtree in Zimbabwe. About 200 kilometres of the mainline track was recently relaid,

the signalling system along the entire network upgraded, and a 165-kilometre track completed to connect Francistown with the Makgadikgadi region's Sowa Pan soda-ash enterprise. New freight termini are planned for Francistown and Gaborone. Proposals for a trans-Kalahari railway through central Botswana and Namibia could be revived (they were shelved during Namibia's liberation struggle) to provide alternative access routes to world markets via the Atlantic seaboard.

Botswana Railways, which became independent of the National Railways of Zimbabwe in 1987, operates what was until recently Southern Africa's only fleet of entirely air-conditioned coaches. Rail journeys, now that the new track is complete, are much quicker than they used to be: speeds of between 120 and 150 km/h are envisaged, reducing travelling time between Gaborone and Francistown to under four hours.

Airways

Air Botswana is a busy little carrier that operates a regional network embracing Johannesburg (South Africa), Harare, Victoria Falls (Zimbabwe), Lusaka (Zambia), Maputo (Mozambique),

Nairobi (Kenya), Entebbe (Uganda), Maseru (Lesotho) and Manzini (Swaziland). The airline's distinctively blue-and-white, high-wing aircraft also provide domestic services that take in, among other centres, Maun, gateway to the Okavango Delta (three flights a week); Kasane, close to the Chobe park's eastern boundary, with connections to Victoria Falls in Zimbabwe; Tuli, and Selebi-Phikwe. The short-haul fleet includes Franco-Italian ATR-42 turbo-props and the splendid BAe 142, the world's quietest jetliner.

Air Botswana's headquarters are at Gaborone's Sir Seretse Khama international airport, the country's principal point of entry, which also plays host to British Airways, UTA (French), Zambia Airways, Air Malawi, Kenya Airlines, Air Tanzania, Lesotho Airways, and Comair (which recently took over from South African Airways as the official South African carrier on the Botswana route). Visitor facilities at the Gaborone airport include bank and *bureau de change*, duty-free shop, post office, book and curio store, bar, coffee shop and car rental booths. Air Botswana's office building is a rather eye-catching affair of two-storey octagonal wings radiating out from open spaces graced by gardens and fountains.

There are regional airports at Francistown, Kasane (recently upgraded), Maun, Tuli and Selebi-Phikwe. Among smaller airlines and charter firms that ply the domestic routes is Okavango Air, which has expanded into the pressurised turbine market. Many of the individual tourist lodges have their own airstrips.

Telecommunications

The national network is being modernized with the installation of a sophisticated digital microwave system that allows international direct dialling, and with the extension of trunk routes to widen the scope of automatic services. Telex and facsimile transmission facilities are widely available in the relatively densely populated eastern region, but communications, understandably, remain problematic in some of the remoter areas.

Passengers board an Air Botswana jetliner at the Seretse Khama International Airport in Gaborone for the next leg of their African safari.

WILD KINGDOM

An impressive array of game parks and reserves and, most especially, the splendid wetlands of the Okavango Delta comprise Botswana's principal tourist attractions. The statistical picture reveals that the country is home – though in many instances a precarious home – to 164 species of mammal, 157 of reptile, 80 of fish, 540 of bird and to uncountable different kinds of plant and insect.

Despite the magnificence of its natural heritage, however, Botswana's tourism industry is relatively young. Practically nothing was done to encourage visitors in the pre-independence era, and since then the wider region's troubled political climate – notably the brutal bush war that devastated Zimbabwe to the northeast, the low-intensity struggle for freedom in South Africa, and the unwelcome overspill from both these convulsions – discouraged the international traveller. And until Botswana's new diamond mines began to yield their full bounty there was precious little money to spare for tourist infrastructure. The very first commercial venue made its appearance only in the late 1960s.

The travelling world, however, has now 'discovered' this most fascinating of lands, and over the past few years holiday-makers have been arriving in increasing numbers, prompting an explosive expansion of amenities – new hotels, resorts, game lodges, fishing camps, safari packages – and the intending visitor now has a wide and inviting choice of options.

Not that the tourism drive is aimed at the mass market. On the contrary, it is generally recognized that Botswana's wilderness areas, vast though they are and rugged though they may appear, are environmentally fragile, the balance within the ecosystems easily upset and highly vulnerable to the human presence. Official policy, therefore, is designed to encourage the low-volume, high-cost trade, and facilities tend to be exclusive (though, let it be said, not especially luxurious) and expensive.

Essentially, the country offers two kinds of wilderness holiday:

The luxurious Chobe Game Lodge in the Chobe National Park is one of the most exclusive and comfortable of Africa's safari destinations.

The lodge safari

The Okavango swampland and its neighbouring Moremi reserve, the game-filled Chobe park to the north and, to a lesser extent, the Tuli area in the east are all served by scores of private wilderness venues.

In most instances, do not expect five-star luxury, whatever the brochures say. The majority of lodges are small (eight to sixteen guests), informal and companionable; some are no more than clusters of tents that are usually spacious and cosily, if somewhat functionally, fitted out; others offer more permanent accommodation ranging from the basic hut to the roomy chalet with all the modern conveniences. Cuisine varies from the deliciously imaginative to food that is designed to sustain rather than please; sanitation arrangements from the communal and primitive to the private and waterborne.

Generally speaking, the smaller the lodge the more personalized the service. Each, though, has its own, very distinct personality – a lack of sameness that is part of the collective charm of these places – and its special attractions: the camp's setting may be unusually beautiful (most of Botswana's commercial lodges, especially those of the northern wetlands, have been cleverly sited and their surrounds are both secluded and lovely); perhaps the area is notable for the fishing, or the birding, or the good

game-viewing it affords. Or it may be ecologically diverse, sustaining a wide and fascinating variety of animal, bird and plant life. A relatively new phenomenon in Botswana is the larger, more sophisticated wilderness establishment that falls somewhere between a safari lodge and an upmarket country hotel/resort complex. This kind of enterprise, though, is still a rarity; most safari venues remain modest in size and unpretentious in character.

Camp routine is casual and undemanding. Much of the day, all but the hottest hours, is spent exploring the wilderness in the company of a professional guide who is skilled in bushcraft and knows a great deal about the lore of the wild. One covers the terrain either on foot or, more usually, in an open, customized four-wheel-drive vehicle, or perhaps in combination of the two. The dug-out canoe, or *mokoro*, and the floating pontoon are the favoured and sometimes the only possible means of transport in the Delta region. One or two of the camps offer exploratory trips by light aircraft. Back at base (and after a much-needed shower or a refreshing dip in the pool) guests foregather for drinks, which are taken in that magical hour when the sun dips low and the golden light spreads, before proceeding to the traditional barbecue dinner. This is known locally as a *braaivleis* (or simply 'braai') and is a marvellously sociable affair of tasty food (grilled venison invariably features during the hunting season), good cheer and animated conversation.

Pretty well all the lodges are associated with and some are owned and run by commercial safari firms. Although one can embark on an independent tour of a region, bear in mind that travelling conditions and access can be difficult, and that it's a lot less troublesome, often cheaper and generally more rewarding to invest in an organized package excursion. The safari operator will know the area intimately, can provide a comforting degree of personal service, and will make sure that you extract the very most from your bush holiday. Moreover, packages invariably take in more than one lodge and sometimes more than one region, so offering the kind of environmental variety that would be difficult to experience if you were going it alone and had limited time at your disposal.

The mobile safari

A number of commercial operators run mobile safaris which, as their name suggests, involve organized treks through the wilderness – on foot or by four-wheel-drive, boat, on horseback or by some other means of locomotion (including, in one notable instance, by elephant) – as a member of a conducted party. Many of the outfits cater for special interests – for bird-lovers, keen photographers, amateur botanists, sporting anglers and so forth. One camps out in the bush, or at a public

A group of holidaymakers view a vast herd of Cape Buffalo from atop their four-wheel drive safari vehicle on the banks of the Chobe River.

The helicopter is a recent innovation in game viewing in Botswana .

park campsite, or overnights at one or more of the permanent venues. Generally speaking, this kind of expedition is less expensive than the more static lodge safari, though costs vary a lot from one to another: at one end of the scale are operators who pamper their guests; at the other, trailists are expected to rough it, and to help with the chores.

Viewing the wildlife

One's venture into the Botswana wilderness will undoubtedly prove an exhilarating experience, but first-time visitors will be entering an alien and perhaps confusing world, so a few preparatory pointers may be helpful, especially to the independent traveller (members of safari groups will be shown the ropes, and generally looked after very well, by their hosts).

Remember that parks and reserves

have been established for the protection of the wildlife, a generic term that encompasses *all* of its living things – animals, birds, reptiles, fish, insects, trees, shrubs, grasses. Here, in the wilderness of Botswana, it is you who are the intruder, your presence a privilege. Don't pollute the countryside with litter (keep a plastic bag in your vehicle for rubbish); stick to the designated roads and tracks.

Get to know something of the habits and habitats of the wildlife before your departure for Botswana, and arm yourself with a good guidebook. Elephant, lion, buffalo, hippo, crocodile, zebra, wildebeest, gemsbok, fish eagle, vulture – each has its own favoured area and daily routine.

Game-viewing is usually at its best during the dry season – in winter (May to August) and in the hot springtime months of September and October, when the animals are concentrated near river, pool and waterhole. The chances of spotting lion are better just after sunrise than at other times. A well-chosen vantage point tends to be more rewarding than the exploratory drive, a point to remember if the Chobe park is your destination. In summer most of the game tends to lie up during the heat of the day (and so do the majority of visitors), so the recommended times to set out on drives are the early mornings (at or soon after first light) and late afternoons. Elephants, though, are wide awake and active in and around the rivers in the hotter hours.

Approach big game with caution; don't make any unnecessary movement or noise, and be prepared to drive on quickly if warning signs appear (if, for instance, an elephant turns head-on to you and flaps its ears). Keep down-wind of your 'quarry' if possible; remember that just about any wild creature can be dangerous if startled, irritated or, most importantly, cornered. Do not under any circumstances cut off an animal's line of retreat; in the northern wetlands, hippos can be a special hazard if their escape route to water is blocked.

If you have a choice of vehicle, bear in mind that a minibus is ideally suited to game-viewing. Many of Botswana's wilderness areas, though, are too rugged and undeveloped for anything short of a four-wheel-drive. If you're on a family or party trip, take along more than one pair of binoculars: having to share, particularly when something really special comes into view, can lead to irritation and argument. Ensure that camera cases are well padded and dust-proof; take along a good supply of film; remember that light is at its best in the early mornings and early evenings and that heat-haze is a problem during the hours between.

Preparing for the trip

Travel light: nobody dresses up in Botswana, least of all on safari; informality and practicality are the key-words, even in the most well-founded and sophisticated of lodges. Shirts and shorts (for men) and shirts/blouses and skirts/shorts (for women) are customary daytime wear; jeans and hard-wearing trousers are valid alternatives. In the game areas, avoid bright colours and white – they are difficult to keep clean, look out of place and, so it's said, tend to attract the now largely eradicated tsetse fly, a nasty little creature whose bite is both painful and capable of transmitting sleeping sickness (easily cured these days but, still, something to be avoided). Neutral hues – khaki, dull greens and browns – are best for your excursions through Kalahari, Okavango swampland and bush country. For walking – which is a standard part of the routine in both the Delta (the islands aren't, of course, accessible to vehicles; one gets there by *mokoro* or other craft and explores on foot) and to a lesser extent the Chobe regions – you'll need a pair of hard-wearing, worn-in shoes, preferably of the ankle variety for protection against scratches, stings and bites. Around camp one wears ordinary shoes, sandals, sneakers or 'slops'.

Sun-hats should shade the neck as well as the face. Botswana's winter nights, as we've noted, are chilly and often bitter – there aren't any clouds to keep in the heat of daytime – so take along a warm sweater, tracksuit or anorak, and a lighter jersey for the sunrise and sunset hours. Among other items to pack are a swimming costume, personal toiletries that include a good barrier cream and lip salve, sunglasses (not a cheap pair), insect repellent, and

Inexperienced travellers should approach big game with caution – and take good heed of warning signals put out by angry animals!

flashlight (fitted with new batteries).

Keep your passport with you at all times – and, if you're motoring, your driver's licence. Foreign licences are valid in Botswana for six months provided they are printed in English or accompanied by a certified translation; alternatively, apply for an International Driving Permit (the procedure is simple and inexpensive). You'll also need third-party insurance cover, which can be bought at the point of entry.

The general speed limit on the open tarred road is 120 km/h. If you intend exploring the Kalahari regions, and your route takes you away from the main highway, leave word behind of your destination and estimated time of arrival, and carry a good stock of spares, extra fuel, and plenty of water.

Health and other hazards

Malaria is a potential problem, especially during the summer months in the northern wetlands – the Delta and around the Linyanti-Chobe river reaches. In some areas mosquitoes have become resistant to certain common drugs. Take a course of anti-malaria tablets before departure; prophylactics are available, without prescription, in pharmacies throughout Southern Africa. Tell the pharmacist which specific regions you intend visiting.

A lesser and easily avoidable risk is bilharzia, also known as schistosomiasis, a waterborne and debilitating disease caused by a parasitical worm that inhabits the Delta and the northern rivers. The transmission cycle is complex and, to the naturalists, fascinating: after developing its larval stage in a water-snail, the bilharzia fluke may penetrate the skin of a person entering the water, later attacking the bladder, liver and kidneys. The eggs then leave the human body in the waste products, but will hatch only if they're discharged into fresh water, where the hatchlings will swim around until they find another snail host. When diagnosed – which can be quite difficult, because the symptoms tend to be rather vague – the disease readily responds to drugs. Be on your guard when out in the wilderness; do not swim in or even come into contact with still water (along river-

Viewing game from the water is just one of the exciting options available to visitors to Botswana. Here a group from Chobe Chilwero camp venture close to a pod of hippo in the Chobe River.

banks and in inlets, lagoons and dams) unless there are clear assurances that it is bilharzia-free.

Botswana has its fair share of creepies and crawlies, some of which can inflict a nasty bite or sting. The southern subcontinent is home to around 115 species of snake, about a quarter of them dangerous (though very seldom fatal) to man. The venom may be haemotoxic (affecting the blood vessels), neurotoxic (affecting the nervous system) or cytotoxic (attacking the body's cells). Snakes, however, are shy creatures, and will slide out of the way when they sense your presence (they should be allowed to do so), only striking if suddenly disturbed or provoked. Among the more notable front-fanged species are the mambas, cobras and adders; back-fanged varieties include the boomslang and birdsnake, both highly poisonous but, because their fangs are too awkwardly positioned to allow them a good grip, they very rarely cause serious injury. Anti-snakebite serum (to be used only in emergencies) is widely available in Botswana; snakebite kits can be bought at pharmacies.

About 5 000 or so types of spider and

scorpion (both are classed as arachnids) can be found in Southern Africa, a goodly percentage of them in Botswana. Many of the former will bite if provoked but, again, few are really dangerous. The most notable exception is Latrodectus, or the button spider. All scorpion venom is toxic to the nervous system, painfully but usually, in Southern Africa, not fatally so. Most of the 175-odd species occur in the hot, dry regions – the deserts of Namibia and the Kalahari sandveld of Botswana.

Finally, be wary of a small, red, hard-backed tick in the northern bush areas. These tiny parasites – which should not be confused with the much larger dog or sheep tick – can, if infected, transmit the typhus-type tickbite fever. Symptoms are very much like those of malaria, but with the added discomforts of a bad neck ache and headache. If you see such a creature on your skin, don't pull or brush it off (the head will remain embedded) but rather smother it with ointment or other covering. Tickbite fever is treatable and, although unpleasant, usually causes no lasting harm (though in rare cases it can lead to heart damage).

The Okavango Delta

The Okavango River rises in the far-off uplands of Angola from where it embarks on a 1 600-kilometre journey south-eastwards, flowing across Namibia's Caprivi region and into Botswana, where it divides into a number of lesser watercourses. These ribbon-like extensions then make their way into the immensity of the Kalahari to part again into a myriad channels, the whole forming a vast and wondrously luxuriant delta of fertile floodplain and riverine forest, reed and papyrus bed, ox-bow lake, lagoon and an intricate network of waterways that embrace more than a thousand wooded islands.

Most of the latter are small, many of them no more than giant mounds of sandy earth created by termites (commonly though incorrectly known as 'white ants') and extensive enough, just, to support a mantle of undergrowth and a couple of palm trees. Others are substantial expanses of dry land, thickly forested and home to a splendid diver-

rob herons and cormorants of their catches, steal their eggs and kill their hatchlings, occasionally hunt other waterbirds, take frogs, insects and a variety of land creatures ranging from rock rabbits to monitor lizards and small monkeys, and even resort to scavenging.

But fascinating though it is, the Delta's wildlife is just one of the elements that make of the region a paradise for the photographer and naturalist, the fisherman and the lover of peace and seclusion. The brooding silence of the waterways, the dense and mysterious beds of papyrus, the quiet rustle of a *mokoro* as it noses its way through the reeds, the scent of the water lilies, the humid heat of the day, the coolness of the evening and the splendour of its sunset – these are the things that, together with the animals and birds, combine to create a total experience, a composite that remains in the memory long after one has departed this enchanting land.

Moving around the Delta Although the swamps have been charted, the network of channels is so intricate, so obscured by vegetation and indeed so impermanent (topography is affected by, among other things, the extent and nature of the floodwaters) that only those who claim long familiarity with its complexities are able to find their way around with confidence. Some sections of the Delta, notably around Maun and on or near the fringes of the swamplands, are accessible to four-wheel-drive vehicles, but all in all intending visitors would be wise to book their trip through one or other of the many safari firms operating in the region. As we've noted, these outfits are familiar with the terrain, handle all the arrangements, and provide an attractive range of services: travel to and accommodation at Maun, transport to the lodge by either light aircraft, vehicle or boat (or a combination of these), food, drink and a comfortable bed, professional guides to take you on walking, game-viewing, photographic, fishing and sight-seeing expeditions, and so forth.

One uses various means of locomotion to get around the Delta, among them powerboat (increasingly frowned upon by the environmentalists), conventional canoe and aircraft. Some of the lodges operate pontoons – large, double-deck craft that fall somewhere between a game-viewing platform and a houseboat, and which drift lazily along the waterways to provide the most relaxing of outings. Horseback trails are offered by one or two enterprises. And one especially enterprising firm (Ker and Downey) runs elephant safaris: trail parties of up to ten people set out on elephant back, with several juvenile pachyderms in tow, to explore the wilderness of grassland and island-studded floodplain. The trip takes five days, the group overnighting at a comfortable tented camp or at one or more of the permanent lodges. Some of the elephants – Abu is the senior animal – belonged to the American circus world until the late 1980s, when they were brought back to their ancestral home by author and naturalist Randall Moore and patiently retrained to carry riders through the great sunlit spaces. For all their sophisticated upbringing, they belong naturally to the African bush, and they move with surprising assurance and gentleness through it.

The most usual and undoubtedly the most environmentally friendly way of seeing this magical land, though, is by *mokoro* (plural: *mekoro),* the traditional dug-out canoe: swift, silent, unobtrusive, the craft skims lighly over the surface to provide a memorable close-encounter experience of Africa at its pristine best.

Peoples of the waterways The traditional *mokoro* is piloted along the waterways, with remarkable expertise, by an African poler who will almost certainly belong to either the Bayei or the Hambukushu groups.

Neither of these peoples has close historical ties to the Tswana: both originally hail from the lands to the north, beyond the Linyanti-Chobe River, moving south in the 18th century to escape oppression by the Lozi of the vast floodplains of Barotseland in the west of today's Zambia. The Bayei were the first to arrive, settling in the Delta area as far south as Lake Ngami in the 1750s. They, and to a lesser extent the Hambukushu who followed them, were river folk and farmers rather than herders, garnering riverine plants during the floods, tilling the floodplains when these receded but, above all, fishing and hunting for hippo in the Delta's waters.

The Bayei tended to remain near the shallows, catching their fish in several different ways but most often with traps fashioned from reed fences and baskets.

Drotsky's Cabins, near Shakawe in the Okavango Panhandle, offer overnight excursions into the Delta in specially equipped Leisureliner houseboats.

For many birders, Pel's fishing owl is the ultimate sighting. Here Lothar and Milla Svoboda, managers of Shindi Island camp, make it easy for them with their pet bird, one of several bred for study purposes by naturalist Tim Liversedge of Maun.

The Hambukushu, on the other hand, at their most concentrated in the north (around the Panhandle), were more a deep-water people who paddled rather than poled their *mekoro,* or *wato* as their canoes were known, and relied more on the fruits of the soil than on the waters for their food supplies.

Much of the old way of life has survived the centuries, the Hambukushu communities reinforced by the refugees – related peoples – who poured down from Angola during the civil strife of the late 1960s. Many of the newcomers wore traditional garb in which beadwork, coiled copper and brass, skin skirts and long wigs (made from shredded wild sisal plants) featured prominently. Customary dress is still worn on ceremonial and other special occasions; children still fish the shallows in time-honoured fashion, trapping their catch behind a mud dam; their fathers still cast their nets in the deeper, papyrus-fringed channels. And the drums, tall ones called *ngoma* and shorter friction ones called *namangwita,* still beat in unison around the small, reed-built Hambukushu settlements to thank and propitiate both God (*Nyambi*) and the ancestral spirits.

Camps and lodges In the early 1990s the Okavango region was served by

more than forty privately run tourist venues, and more were being established by the year. Some of the camps consist of simple reed, pole and thatch structures, others brick under thatch, still others large and airy safari tents; most have *en suite* bathroom facilities, swimming pool, communal dining and relaxation areas, viewing platforms (often doubling as bars) and solar-power electricity.

Conventional accommodation is at present confined to the Maun area in the south (see page 17), where Riley's Hotel plays amiable host to visitors on their way north to the Moremi reserve or north-westwards into the remoter Delta region. Riley's is something of an institution in Botswana, known to and loved by generations of the rugged safari community. On the well-wooded banks of the Thamalakane River not too far away are Sitatunga Lodge, a pleasantly shady and unpretentious place of campsites, serviced chalets and lovely forest surrounds; and, on the other side of Maun, the old-established and charming Crocodile Camp, widely known for its fine food and sociable pub. The camps in the north-western part of the Delta – the region of permanent waters and the Panhandle (the narrow main channel and floodplain of the Okavango River) after it

crosses the Caprivi region– offer several enticing camps, most of which specialize, though not exclusively, in fishing safaris. At Drotsky's Cabins (named after its owners) one can hire a canoe, power-boat or self-contained houseboat and embark on night-time trips (an exhilarating experience) and on conducted excursions to the Tsodilo Hills (see page 18). The region's other venues offer similar attractions; one of the most enchanting is Shindi Camp, tucked away on its own magical island and famed for the fine fishing and even finer birding opportunities it offers.

Also of note are Xaro Lodge, a tented but luxurious camp that caters quite beautifully for the sporting fisherman, and Nxamaseri Lodge, an angler's (and bird-lover's) paradise set on an island graced by giant ebony trees. Here the views, over lily-covered waterway to lushly wooded islet and riverine forest, are memorable. Shindi Camp also has its own island (fine birding here), as does Jedibe Island Camp, which incorporates an unusually splendid reed-and-thatch complex of dining room, bar and 'boma' (an open-air barbecue area).

Most of the lodges in the central, eastern and northern Delta are close to the boundaries of the formally proclaimed Moremi santuary (see following section).

Moremi Game Reserve
A large slice of the north-eastern Okavango Delta has been set aside as the Moremi reserve, a marvellously unspoilt 2 000-square-kilometre wilderness that bears testament to the determination of the local Tswana people, and to the vision of conservationists Robert and June Kaye.

During the 1950s and early 1960s there was deep and growing concern, among environmentalists, the authorities and the villagers, over the depletion of the region's precious resources. The game animals were fast disappearing, victims of Tswana hunters who had for decades been assured of an inexhaustible supply of fresh meat, and of the more lethal professional 'white' hunting outfits, mainly safari companies from East Africa in quest of new killing grounds. Encouraged by the Kayes, the

The network of paved roads is fast spreading over Botswana, but once off the beaten track four-wheel drive enthusiasts are kept happy with some gruelling driving and the occasional picturesque mopane pole 'bridge'.

Tswana decided to convert part of their tribal territory into a formal sanctuary – even though this meant, for many of the families, an unsettling move away from their traditional lands. It was a courageous and ground-breaking step: the Moremi, named after a tribal chief, is the first wildlife haven in Southern Africa to have been created by an African community on its own property. Later on, the huge and beautiful wilderness of Chief's Island was added to the reserve and, together, the two tracts were until recently the only formally protected areas within the Okavango Delta.

Moremi is famed for the diversity of its habitats. The reserve extends over both wetland and dry country to form a splendid territorial mix: floodplain and forested island, lily-mantled lagoon, dense papyrus bed, twisty-rooted strangler fig, giant fan-palm and deep-green mopane woodland give way, in the east and north (towards the Chobe National Park; see following section) to riverine acacia and grassland. Most of the wetland's islands are tiny but a few are substantial and one – Chief's – is an enormous expanse of forest and grassland flanked by two largish rivers, the Boro and the Santantadibe.

Wildlife The entire reserve is renowned for the profusion and variety of its animal and bird populations. The wildlife, refreshingly, remains relatively undisturbed: the reserve isn't fenced (though veterinary cordons have been erected some distance away; see page 50) and the big game – huge herds of elephant, of buffalo, zebra and various antelope – migrate freely between the fringes of the wetlands and the great spaces of the Chobe to the north-east; among the more familiar sights are the lechwe, kudu, tsessebe and, most especially, graceful impala in their thousands; less common are reedbuck, bushbuck and waterbuck; baboons are everywhere. And, because of the abundance of plains game, the predators are present in force: lion and leopard, cheetah, wild dog and such smaller nocturnal species as the serval, the caracal and the African wild cat.

The lagoons, their waters covered by lily-pads and pale blue (and at other times yellow or white) flowers, are brightly animated with the sounds and colourful sights of jacana and crested barbet, babbler and hoopoe, pied and malachite kingfisher, marabou stork, egret, reed cormorant, darter, fish eagle, whiskered tern, saddle-billed and yellow-billed stork, glossy and sacred ibis, plover, wood sandpiper, African skimmer, knob-billed and white-faced duck, spurwing, Egyptian and pygmy goose – in all, more than 400 avian species, many of them secretive and elusive, some highly visible. Especially notable are the heronries at Xakanaxa, Gcobega and Gcodikwe, home to squacco, green-backed, rufousbellied, blackheaded, night and purple heron, slaty egret and to a myriad other waterbirds.

Exploring the Moremi The drier months, from about May to November, are the most inviting – in terms of weather, game-viewing and bird-spotting. Getting to the area presents few problems: one can fly in to Maun, hire a four-wheel-drive vehicle and drive up the 100-kilometre road to the reserve's South Gate (the surface tends to be sandy but is otherwise usually in good condition and is being tarred), or motor

The tiny, jewel-like malachite kingfisher is but one of more than 400 bird species identified in the Moremi Game Reserve and its surrounds.

in by way of Francistown and Nata.

The internal route network is a bit restricting, but extensive enough for ordinary tourist purposes: the eastern section of the reserve is traversed by tracks that form a kind of triangle between South Gate, North Gate and, to the west, Third Bridge. These roads are also sandy and, especially during the wet season, challenging: one needs a four-wheel-drive and, even then, it is difficult, sometimes impossible, to negotiate them during periods of heavy rain.

Camps and lodges There is no permanent public accommodation within the formal bounds of the Moremi – a deficiency that is part of a deliberate policy to limit the human presence, to keep the area as pristine as possible. However, four camping venues have been established at the two gates, at Third Bridge to the west and at nearby Xakanaxa. The sites are fairly basic: visitor facilities amount to little more than showers and waterborne sanitation, and even these tend to be inadequate during crowded holiday periods.

In striking contrast to the poverty of public amenities, however, is the ring of private lodges and camps established around the fringes of the reserve. At the time of writing there were about twenty of them, each with its own personality. A representative sample would include:

Khwai River Lodge, one of the region's oldest and most charming, its round brick-and-thatch chalets, set beneath a splendid canopy of giant indigenous trees, overlooking the river's floodplain. Elephant and other big game, including the resident hippos, can be viewed in comfort from the lodge's pleasantly lawned grounds. This is one of the six lodges in the Delta and Chobe areas that now belong to the Orient Express-Mount Nelson group and the food, the service and the amenities are, predictably, of an exceptional standard. There is also magnificent bird-watching in and around the lodge's grounds.

Camp Okavango and Camp Moremi. These two top-of-the-range venues are the creation of Jessie Neil, a Californian lady whose good taste, careful attention to detail and deep love of the wilderness are in evidence everywhere (though she herself has departed the scene): cuisine is cordon bleu, the service attentive, the appointments elegant. Okavango nestles among the tall jackalberry and sausage trees of an island among the permanent lagoons and channels of the northern Delta, and water is the focus of visitor activities (exploratory trips by *mokoro*, walks on neighbouring islands, fishing expeditions). Nearby Camp Moremi, on the other hand, is in big-game country. Lion and buffalo are especially prominent, and you can see these and much else on the conducted drives taken in quite beautifully maintained safari vehicles. The camp's most striking feature is its central complex of dining, bar and lounge areas, timbered and raised high above the lovely waters of Xakanaxa lagoon; accommodation is in luxurious East African-style tents; guests are ferried from one camp to another by boat.

Oddballs, on the south-western corner of Chief's Island, is one of the few private camps in the Delta that offers self-catering accommodation, providing a relatively inexpensive alternative to the more usual luxury establishment. Once a focus for the back-packing fraternity (which, with the hefty 600 per cent increase in park entry fees in 1989, has largely disappeared from the Botswana wilderness scene), it was upgraded fairly recently but is still a casual, undemanding kind of place and a thoroughly enjoyable base from which to explore the waters. Its rather curious name is apt enough in some respects: Oddballs does tend to attract a sprinkling of eccentric, larger-than-life characters.

Mombo Camp, on the northern tip of Chief's Island, is renowned for its big herds of ungulates, its predators (all the major ones), and for its three resident packs of the endangered, much-maligned and in many ways beautiful Cape hunting dog (or wild dog). The classic documentary *Sisterhood* was filmed at the camp. This is a region of both land and water, and Mombo camp offers a quite exceptional all-round wilderness experience.

Xakanaxa Camp, on the exquisite lagoon of that name, has more of the old Africa about it than most: its East African-type tents, illuminated at night by hurricane lamps, are raised on platforms shaded by tall and handsome trees. The waters here attract nesting colonies of storks in springtime.

Also on the lagoon is Camp Okuti, a small (14-guest), unpretentious and pleasantly shady lodge that sets out to provide a 'special African experience', and succeeds quite admirably in doing so. Okuti is known for the warmth with which its guests are generally received and looked after.

San-ta-Wani Safari Lodge, close to the Moremi's South Gate, is enchantingly surrounded by lofty trees and wild flowers (the grounds are lovingly tended, by a blind gardener). The area is rich in game, though the animals – elephant and buffalo among them – are said to be rather skittish (hunters are active in the area). Meals are most often enjoyed in the reed-enclosed boma.

Delta Camp, tucked away among the trees of the Boro river-bank, is one of the most attractive and peaceful of all the lodges. The owners have banished powerboats from their corner of the swamplands – part of a private campaign against noise pollution – in favour of the graceful *mokoro*, whose polers are especially expert and knowledgeable. They take you out on extended exploratory excursions through the channels, stopping at sunset to pitch the tents, to cook a surprisingly imaginative campfire meal, and to sit beneath the stars and share their wisdom with you.

Xaxaba, among several camps just to the south of Chief's Island, has an especially lovely setting, seen at its best perhaps when one relaxes with a long drink to hand and the last of the sun casting

One of the smallest of all Botswana's camps, Selinda overlooks the Selinda spillway where water runs from the Linyanti River to the Okavango in some years, while in others this flow may be reversed.

its soft light over the waters. One of the most popular of the camps, Xaxaba offers its guests *mokoro* and powerboat trips, game-viewing cruises aboard a pontoon, walking trails (there's splendid birding in the area), fishing expeditions, and sightseeing by light aircraft.

Chobe National Park

The Linyanti-Chobe river system marks Botswana's northern border, dividing the country from Namibia's fairly heavily cultivated Caprivi Strip. The terrain on the Botswana side, most of it proclaimed as the Chobe National Park, thus effectively forms a kind of catchment area for the great herds of plains game that trek north from the arid north-central parts of the country. The result is a remarkable richness of wildlife, a veritable treasure-house of animals on display for the naturalist to study and the safari enthusiast to enjoy.

The park covers a magnificent 11 000 square kilometres of wilderness, its diverse components taking in river and floodplain, grassland, natural pan, seasonal swamp, patches of mopane, teak, acacia and kiaat woodland and extensive areas of flat, rather featureless Kalahari semi-desert.

For much of the year most of the pans remain empty, but the river is perennial and life-sustaining, and there are a number of waterholes scattered around the park's harsh, dust-dry central and southern parts. During the second half of each year the Linyanti-Chobe floods, spilling some of its precious water southwards, very occasionally as far as the Savuti Channel to filter into the game-rich Savuti marshlands.

Wildlife The park's water resources, though by no means generous, are at least adequate and, together with the leaves and shoots of the woodlands and the sweet grasses of the plains, they sustain a wonderful profusion of animal and bird life. The elephant of the region – they number an estimated 35 000 head, which is the largest concentration to be found in any of Africa's national parks – together with the buffalo, huge herds of them, migrate northwards to congregate around the rivers and flood-

plains. The aggregations are an unforgettable sight, especially at the going down of the sun, when the land and its multitude of animals are bathed in the reds and golds of a dying day. Other creatures abound in the Chobe's well-watered northern section, among them crocodile and hippo and various antelope, including the red lechwe, the Chobe bushbuck (more brightly coloured than its cousins elsewhere) and the relatively rare puku. This last-named, which is at the southern limit of its range in and around the Chobe's Puku Flats, was once fairly prolific farther north, in the region stretching from eastern Caprivi to south-western Tanzania, but its numbers have been drastically reduced by human settlement and hunting. It is rather similar in appearance to but smaller than the lechwe; in habit it resembles the waterbuck, though different in its willingness to mingle with impala and other bovids.

At one time the park was thought to offer ideal habitats for white rhino, and quite a few were brought in from the distant Zululand reserves, but as in so many other regions of Africa the poachers have won the day and the animals were, at the time of writing, on the edge

Lloyd Wilmot – 'Mr Savute' – and friends. Lloyd, one of the region's better known characters, operates a safari camp in the heart of big game country on the Savute Channel in the Chobe National Park.

of local extinction.

At certain times of the year the big game is as prolific, if not even more so, in the Savute as in the riverine area of the Chobe. Here the Savute Channel, so shallow as to be virtually indiscernible, connects the northern river with the Mababe Depression, once a great lake but now, for all but a few brief periods during each decade, a vast grassland plain stretching to far horizons, treeless, seemingly devoid of life. But with the rains come the wildebeest, the giraffe, the tsessebe and the zebra (up to 25 000 of these migrate down from the north), elephant, buffalo and much else. This enormous influx of game provides easy pickings for the carnivores, and the area is renowned for its lion, leopard and cheetah, hyaena and wild dog. At the junction of channel and depression is the Savute Marsh, also dry for most of the time but now and again moistened by the southward moving waters.

The Chobe's avifauna, especially the birds of the northern wetlands, is quite superb: around 460 species have been identified, among them such notables as the reed cormorant, the saddlebilled and marabou stork, the purple heron, Egyptian goose, egret and ibis, kingfisher, firefinch and francolin, weavers, wagtails, hoopoes, hornbills and a host of busy little bee-eaters.

Travel to and within the Chobe The park's administrative headquarters are in the thriving and rapidly expanding little centre of Kasane, just outside the north-western boundary and to the west of the Kazungula border post. Here there are three hotels and pretty well everything else the undemanding traveller is likely to need. The town is accessible from the south-east (from Gaborone and Francistown via Nata), from Maun and Moremi (the road is rather rugged). There are also trouble-free routes to Namibia's enticing Caprivi region and, after crossing the Zambezi by the Kazungula ferry, to Livingstone and the Victoria Falls (70 kilometres due east, on the border between Zambia and Zimbabwe). The road from Gaborone is now fully tarred; most visitors, however, fly in as guests of one or other

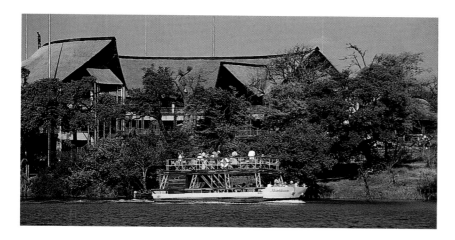

*Cresta Mowana Safari Lodge outside Kasane is architecturally the most spectacular develop-
ment in the country. This multi-million dollar enterprise offers powerboat and houseboat
cruises as well as game drives into the nearby Chobe National Park.*

of the many safari companies that operate in the area.

A small segment of the region – the
35-kilometre stretch of river frontage
running from Kasane westwards to
Ngoma – has been fairly extensively and
most attractively developed for tourism:
a number of fine private lodges and
hotels have been established along the
river, and the connecting road, though it
can be difficult in wet weather and very
sandy in dry, is usually in good enough
condition for ordinary saloon cars.
However, one needs a four-wheel-drive
to explore the rest of the Chobe's great
wilderness spaces: surfaces are rough,
and can be very treacherous.

The park is open throughout the year,
though the areas around the Mababe
Depression and Savute Channel can be
virtually impassable during the rainy
season. For light aircraft, there are two
airstrips within the Chobe park (at
Linyanti and Savute).

Camps, lodges and hotels Like the
Moremi reserve – and indeed in common with all of Botswana's wilderness
areas – the Chobe's public amenities
are few, far between and rudimentary.
There are three public campsites: two
close to the river in the north-west and
one at Savute in the west-central parts.
Visitors must bring all their provisions
with them; facilities are more or less limited to communal ablution blocks.

Private accommodation, though, is in
an entirely different class. About 11 kilometres from Kasane and in the park is
the Chobe Game Lodge, a sophisticated
five-star hotel-resort complex that plays
host to a cosmopolitan and in some
instances celebrated clientele (Elizabeth
Taylor and Richard Burton spent their
second honeymoon in one of its luxurious suites). The lodge's architecture is
unusual, gracefully Moroccan in style
and at odds perhaps with its setting of
raw Africa, but the contrast appeals
rather than offends. Most of the guests
are there for the game-viewing, of
course, and are conducted on expeditions by safari vehicle, by light aircraft or
helicopter (on offer are trips to the
Victoria Falls, the Okavango Delta and
Moremi as well as to Chobe's Savute
region), and by boat along the waterways. There's also an evening cruise on a
two-deck barge that makes its leisurely
way past the river-banks and their teeming wildlife. The sunsets from here are
quite stunning.

River-boat excursions are also laid on
by the nearby Chobe Safari Lodge, an
older-established, unpretentious and
comfortably homely place that is patron-
ized both by a family-type clientele and
by game hunters, safari guides, bush
pilots and sundry colourful characters
with stories to tell. Among other river-

side venues between Kasane and the
park gate are:

Kubu Lodge, at Kazungula, 9 kilometres east of Kasane: a charming
cluster of Swiss-type, timber-and-thatch
chalets set high above the water among
tall jacaranda and flamboyant trees.
Kubu's pride is its split-level restaurant
and bar complex, from which there are
glorious sunset views.

Chobe Chilwero, between Kasane and
the park's gate, also offers splendid vis-
tas: it's been sited atop a 100-metre-
high hill overlooking the river and its
game-rich floodplain. The game guides
here are quite outstanding, especially
when it comes to birding. The lodge's
A-frame bungalows are comfortable. The
cuisine, enjoyed around an enormous
kiaat dining table, is outstanding.

Cresta Mowana Safari Lodge, a
recently built luxury hotel complex, is
the largest and probably the most
sophisticated of the venues: the two-
storey building, beautifully designed to
blend with its riverside setting, has more
than a hundred bedrooms (each with its
private balcony), a conference centre
and shops. It offers two swimming pools,
fine à la carte fare in its restaurant, and
a host of visitor activities ranging from
game-viewing excursions by safari
vehicle, boat, light aircraft and helicopter to nature walks, kayaking expeditions and day-trips to the Victoria Falls.

Less upmarket, perhaps closer to the
'authentic' Africa, are the farther-flung
private camps. The Linyanti has an
exquisite setting – reminiscent of the
Okavango Delta at its most entrancing –
on the Linyanti River's floodplain.
Selinda Bush Camp, its smaller sister, is
fairly close by, in an area graced by
lagoon, palm-fringed island and deep-
green riverine forest. Even more ruggedly remote are the two tented camps in
the semi-arid Savute area – Lloyd's and
Savuti South, though this last has been
taken over by the Orient Express-Mount
Nelson enterprise and guests are, if not
pampered, unusually well looked after.
These are places for the really discerning
wildlife enthusiast: there aren't many
frills, but the game-viewing is magnificent and the complete wilderness experience memorable.

The Makgadikgadi region

To the south-east of the Okavango swamplands, and precariously linked to them by the mostly dry Boteti River, are two of the world's largest salt pans, enormous shallow basins scraped out of the arid northern sands of the Kalahari. The depressions were once part of an inland sea the size of and perhaps even bigger than East Africa's Lake Victoria. For millennia the region was covered by a dense mantle of vegetation and populated by a wondrous array of wildlife, but seismic disturbances diminished the flow from the northern rivers, leaving a shallow expanse of water which soon evaporated in the searing heat to create a wilderness of salt and clay. Or so the scientists believe, and their theory receives modest support from the languages of the area: one place-name refers to reeds, another to rhinoceros. Indeed the very words Kgalagadi and Kalahari are derived from the Setswana phrase for 'to dry up'.

Ntwetwe and Sowa are the largest of a series of pans that also includes Nxai to the north and Mopipi and Lake Xau to the south. They are flat, featureless, for the most part dust-dry expanses, blindingly white in the relentless harshness of the African sun and, like Namibia's Etosha region far to the west, deceptively animated by mirages that dance and shimmer in the burning air. Here and there, though, the flatness of the land-scape is interrupted by 'islands' of trees, pockets of richer soil which have captured and sustained thickets of vegetation that form tiny but coherent wildlife habitats. And when the brief rains come the entire area is transformed: the surfaces are covered by thin sheets of water, and the desert comes alive: flamingoes, pelicans, waders and all manner of other waterfowl flock to the area in their tens of thousands. One sighting alone is reported to have encompassed an incredible million and more birds.

Animals also congregate at these times. The general region is rich in plains game – though poaching for profit and hunting for food and trophies is a serious problem outside the relatively small conservation areas that have been formally proclaimed. The wildlife migrates according to the dictates of season and the availability of food and water resources: in dry periods the herds – notably wildebeest and zebra – tend to gather in the open countryside to the west, but move eastwards when the rains fall. The northern parts – the broad, mokolane palm-studded grasslands between Ntwetwe and Nxai – are especially well endowed. Here are springbok and hardy, drought-adapted gemsbok, blue wildebeest, red hartebeest, teeming plains zebra and their attendant predators – the big cats, jackal and wild dog, the spotted and the rare brown hyaena.

Only a small part of the Ntwetwe has been set aside for conservation: its western tip forms part of the 6 800-square-kilometre Makgadikgadi Pans Game Reserve. The Nxai Pan area to the north was recently incorporated within the Makgadikgadi reserve. In addition, a 310-square-kilometre portion of the Nata delta to the west – the area at the junction of the sporadically flowing fresh-water Nata River and saline Sowa Pan – has been proclaimed (a local, private initiative) as the Nata Sanctuary. In times of flood the usually dry and deso-late-looking terrain here becomes a magical, island-graced waterfowl habitat.

By contrast, the whole of the Nxai Pan, together with a number of smaller depressions and a group of large old

Kubu Island, locally known as The Lost City, rises like a spectre from the surrealistic salt flats of the Makgadikgadi Pans.

Artist and explorer Thomas Baines painted this cluster of baobab trees when he passed through the area in 1862, and it has scarcely changed in shape or size since.

trees known as Baines' Baobabs (they were painted by the respected traveller-artist in 1862 and, according to photographs, have scarcely changed in size and shape since), and alternatively as the 'Sleeping Sisters', lay within the Nxai Pan National Park until its absorption into the Makgadikgadi reserve. The area is misleadingly named: it, too, was once part of a wetland wilderness but today it's entirely grassed over, the flat monotony of the terrain relieved by swathes of mopane woodland and by thickets of acacia. At Nxai the animal populations are similar to those of the Makgadikgadi pans but complemented by giraffe and, just after the first rains fall, by a small number of elephant from the north. Bird life is impressive: about 250 species, among them some notable raptors, have been recorded.

Travelling around the region The Makgadikgadi and Nxai areas are connected by road to Francistown (via the tiny centres of Gweta and Nata: see further on) in the east and to Maun in the west. The main access road is in excellent condition, but a four-wheel-drive is recommended, at times even essential,

for getting around the wider Makgadikgadi region.

Best months to visit the Makgadikgadi pans are April through to July, after which the game animals move off to the Boteti River. Nxai, on the other hand, is at its most rewarding between December and April, when the wildlife is attracted to the rain-enriched grass-lands. Visitor facilities are almost non-existent; a four-wheel-drive vehicle is essential; travellers should bring everything they will or might need with them – tents, bedding, food, vehicle spares, extra fuel, plenty of drinking water.

Among other points to remember: the roads that cross the pans themselves are more or less risk-free, but one shouldn't stray – the briny crust of the pans is hard but not unbreakable, and vehicles can sink to their axles and beyond in the soft sub-surface. The Makgadikgadi and Nxai reserves boast a network of unsign-posted tracks, and with a little prepara-tory research one can find one's way around fairly easily, but an experienced guide is recommended for travel outside the proclaimed areas. Walking is not permitted: the terrain is largely feature-less and it's only too easy to get lost.

Predators are an added hazard. However, visitors are permitted and even encouraged to walk in the small Nata Sanctuary (a bird-viewing hide has been erected on the eastern shore of Sowa Pan).

Camps and lodges Neither the Makgadikgadi pans nor the Nxai area offers permanent accommodation, though camping grounds have been established in both. Facilities, again, are primitive. The former has three venues: Njuge Hills, in the eastern part of the Ntwetwe Pan, comprises two sites atop a high and ancient dune from which there are fine views of the surrounding flatlands; the sunsets are breathtaking, the silence infinite. The third venue, Xhugama, is a sandy, tree-shaded spot on the Boteti river-bank (the 'water-course' is dry for most of the time). The Nxai area offers two sites, both fairly basic (though they do have ablutions).

Two privately run venues, located near the main highway leading to Maun and the Okavango, provide a lot more comfort and easy access to the pans. Nata Lodge, 10 kilometres south of Nata village, serves as both a welcome stopover for the long-distance traveller and a convenient base from which to explore the Makgadikgadi and, to a lesser extent, the Nxai. Set on the rim of Sowa Pan, the lodge is a cluster of neat and well-appointed A-frame bungalows, restaurant, bar and swimming pool in a most pleasant setting of monkeythorn, marula and palm trees; on offer are four-wheel-drive forays to and across the pans, and excellent birding in the rainy season, when the Nata River floods into Sowa to attract a myriad flamigoes, peli-cans and other aquatic species.

The second establishment, Gweta Safari Lodge, lies just to the north of Ntwetwe and is also strategically sited for those wanting to explore both the pan and the wider area. The 'lodge' is in fact a standard motel, and a very pleas-ant one too: its restaurant offers sustain-ing à la carte fare, the pub is friendly and much favoured by the locals. For guests, there are exhilerating horse-trails and exploratory drives in specially equipped 'all terrain' vehicles.

Mashatu is the largest privately owned game reserve in southern Africa, and home to the world's largest privately conserved elephant population. It also offers unsurpassed luxury and cuisine.

The Tuli region

Far to the south-east of the pans, in the relatively fertile, wedge-shaped area between the Limpopo and Shashe rivers, and fringing Botswana's border with the Transvaal, is what is known as the Tuli Block. The countryside here is ruggedly beautiful, distinguished by starkly shaped granite hills and out-crops, open plains, mopane woodlands and, in the riverine parts, by tall acacia, sycamore fig, winterthorn and nyala-berry (or mashatu) trees. The region is fairly heavily populated, but most of the people live in the urban centres, leaving the land, still rich in wildlife, to sprawl-ing farms and ranches and to one or two extensive private game properties.

Pride of the Tuli region, though, is per-haps Mashatu, the largest privately owned game reserve in Southern Africa and home to the world's largest privately conserved elephant population. The lat-ter, known as the 'relic herds of the Shashe', are remnants of the once-great pachyderm populations of the Limpopo Valley: the animals, mercilessly slaugh-tered for their ivory during the 19th century, became locally extinct and remained so for about 60 years until, in the later 1940s, a few refugee groups began filtering back to the sanctuary of the Tuli enclave. Today Mashatu sup-ports around 700 elephant.

The magnificent Mashatu wilderness occupies some 30 000 hectares of grassland, rocky ridge and narrow flood-plain that, together, sustain a great deal of wildlife beside elephant. Here you'll find giraffe and zebra, the stately eland, impala, steenbok, kudu, bushbuck, waterbuck, lion, leopard, spotted hy-aena, the occasional cheetah, warthog, baboon and a host of smaller, mainly nocturnal mammals. Nearly 400 bird species have been identified in the area. And visitors see all this in style: radio-linked safari vehicles set out at dawn and again at dusk; the Tswana rangers and trackers are superlative guides, pro-foundly knowledgeable about the en-vironment and more than willing to impart their wisdom.

Mashatu falls into the luxury category; its cosmopolitan clientele has two choices of accommodation. The main camp, known as Majale Lodge, compris-es comfortably furnished and thoughtful-ly appointed chalets and rondavels, each with a 'his' and 'hers' bathroom and a shady private verandah with splendid bushveld views. Drinks are enjoyed around the filtered swimming pool and in the bar, which is raised to overlook a waterhole that is illuminated at night; dinner (the menu features delicious ven-ison dishes) is usually taken in the reed-and palm-enclosed boma, which has a game-viewing window. Then there's the tented camp, called Thakadu – a pleas-ant collection of twin-bedded units with *en suite* facilities located in the remote-ness of the reserve's northern section.

Tuli Safari Lodge, close to the South African border, is the third of the region's venues, a splendid place of thatched chalets and a quite beautifully designed central complex that features a glassed-in dining room, an unusual bar (it's been built around a giant tree), patio and filtered pool, the whole embraced by landscaped and lovingly tended grounds. From the patio you look out to a waterfall that is enchantingly floodlit at night, and which attracts a steady parade of animals (klipspringer, bush-buck, sometimes a leopard, and a great many smaller, nocturnal species); the gardens are graced by lush plantings, lawns and by some of the oldest, tallest and most handsome mashatu trees you'll see anywhere. Again, game drives are laid on; among other mammal species in the 7 500-hectare reserve are elephant, lion, hyaena and a variety of antelope. There's also good birding in the area; the impressive raptor population includes snake, fish and black eagle.

The Kalahari reserves

About two-thirds of Botswana, as we've seen, is covered by the reddish sands and sparsely grassed plains of the Kalahari, a desert only in name: forbidding though it appears, it sustains its own, distinctive and in some instances unique animal and plant life. And its hardy human presence as well: the vast, harsh spaces are home to some of the last of the Bushman communities (see page 14), once semi-nomadic hunter-gatherers who until recently managed to resist the pressures and temptations of western culture.

Large parts of the Kalahari – some 75 000 square kilometres in all – have been set aside for conservation. None

Visitors to the Central Kalahari Game Reserve must be totally self-contained, carrying with them all their water, food, fuel and vehicle spares.

are well developed for tourism; the roads (where they exist) are challenging; amenities are minimal. The four protected areas comprise:

Central Kalahari Game Reserve More than 50 000 square kilometres in extent and occupying, as its name suggests, much of the arid central region of the Kalahari, the reserve is the second-biggest conservation area in the world, home to scattered groups of Bushmen, and haven to large (though rapidly declining) numbers of game animals, among them gemsbok and springbok, giraffe, blue wildebeest, eland, red hartebeest, and to such carnivores as lion, leopard, cheetah, hyaena and wild dog. This is an exceptionally dry wilderness – rainfall is rare, and there are no rivers or permanent waterholes – but the wildlife is superbly adapted to the conditions: moisture is obtained from such unlikely sources as the dew-covered night-time plants, the deep roots of succulents and the water-filled tsamma melon and wild cucumber. Moreover, boreholes have recently been sunk. The reserve's Deception Valley has served as home to Mark and Delia Owens, authors of that fascinating and moving book *Cry of the Kalahari*. There were no visitor facilities at the time of writing (1994) – indeed, until recently, entry into the reserve was strictly limited to researchers and to the occasional intrepid camper and mobile safari group. Now there's unrestricted access, and visitors may unfold there where they please until the parks authorities have completed their proposed campsite.

Khutse Game Reserve This forms a 2 600-square-kilometre appendage to the Central Kalahari sanctuary, but is much more accessible to visitors than its huge northern neighbour. The terrain is rugged, made up of broad, sandy, thinly grassed plains, fossil dunes, dry river-beds, scatters of acacia and other drought-resistant trees and, the most distinctive of its physical features, a number of seasonal Kalahari pans, most of them sandy but some shrub- and grass-covered. The depressions were once part of an extensive but now long-

dry river system. Despite its lack of surface water, though, the reserve manages to support flourishing populations of migratory antelope together with their predators. The reserve is accessible from Gaborone via Molepolele and Letlhakeng; the road beyond Letlhakeng is suitable only for four-wheel-drive vehicles; visitors can choose among four demarcated camping sites.

Mabuasehube Game Reserve Located in the far south of the region (it's about 150 kilometres north of the border with South Africa's Cape province), the Mabuasehube is noted for its three large pans, its migratory antelope and its carnivores. The reserve, whose name means 'red earth' in the local language, is for the hardier traveller: the area is immensely isolated, the single track sandy and corrugated, and if you break down there is no one, usually, on whom you can call for help. The best access route is from the northern Cape, via Kuruman and Tsabong (which serves as the border post). The road, which is suitable only for four-wheel-drive vehicles, passes through the reserve to continue on to Tshane and Ghanzi. Again, there is nothing laid on for visitors; provisions and petrol are available at Tsabong, and it's recommended you advise the police there of your itinerary before entering the area.

Gemsbok National Park The ancient bed of the Nosop River delineates part of the border between Botswana and South Africa, and also the technical boundary between the former's Gemsbok National Park and the latter's Kalahari Gemsbok National Park. In ecological terms, however, the two form a single entity, though the 11 000-square-kilometre portion within Botswana hasn't yet been developed for tourism. The terrain is typical of the Kalahari's drier regions; among the more pronounced features are fossil river-beds that slice between the high, red sand dunes. There is access from the Botswana side, but most visitors enter via Twee Rivieren on the South African side, a few through Mata Mata in the Namibian section of the Kalahari.

CONSERVING THE WILDERNESS

On the face of it, Botswana has an admirable record when it comes to environmental protection – an impressive 17 per cent of the country has been set aside in one form or another: as national park land, game reserve or wildlife management area (WMA). And if the aims of the National Conservation Strategy are realized, that figure will rise to a huge 39 per cent.

The authors of the strategy see a strong and clear connection between Botswana's human population explosion and its pressing environmental issues, chief among which are: the depletion of wildlife; depletion of natural woodlands; over-exploitation of veld products; rangeland degradation, and pressure on water resources.

The statistics paint a sombre picture. To take a few examples from a fairly recent survey conducted by the country's Department of Wildlife and National Parks:

• Decline in species numbers over a decade: wildebeest 90 per cent; hartebeest 88 per cent; roan antelope 21 per cent; tsessebe 17 per cent; sable antelope 13 per cent.

• Decline over five years: buffalo 46 per cent; zebra 27 per cent (75 per cent decline over 10 years in the Makgadikgadi area).

But there has already been some progress within the framework of the strategy: the Moremi was recently extended to cover the north-western papyrus swamps (the Xo Flats), and two wildlife areas in other parts of the wider Delta region – the Okavango and Kwando reserves – have been formally proclaimed. In the early 1990s a new, environment-friendly policy was adopted placing heavy emphasis on low-impact, high-value tourism. And so on. The authorities are, obviously, acutely conscious of the need to preserve their country's priceless natural heritage.

But for all that, the wilderness regions of Botswana, and most notably the magnificent Okavango swamplands, are under dire threat from human need, and from human folly. Overstocking and general degradation of adjacent lands has led to a shortage of good grazing, and the Delta's water and the green richness of its floodplains, incongruously luxuriant oases in an otherwise parched countryside, are a standing temptation to the stock farmers.

Cattle are quite clearly the key factor in the conservation equation, but the solutions are anything but simple. Wild ruminants, though immune to the tsetse fly, can pass the deadly nagana virus on to the domestic herds. They can also transit the foot-and-mouth virus to which, again, they are impervious. Botswana's beef industry has been supported by the World Bank (which eventually pulled out because its aid was seen to be counter-productive), by the EEC (which pays 60 per cent above world prices, even though it has a vast stockpile of its own) and by other donors, all of whom are insistent on disease-free beef on the one hand and wildlife protection on the other. So to keep the game in and the cattle out of the Delta, veterinary cordons have been erected to the south and west of the wetland areas.

The move is said to have proved effective, though it took tragic toll of the game from the earliest days of the programme. In 1984, for example, 50 000 migrating wildebeest perished around Lake Xau in the northern Kalahari, channelled into a grassless wilderness by the Kuke fence, and Bushmen have reported that elephant, buffalo, roan and sable, which once roamed the northern Kalahari in their multitudes, have gone from the area. The central Kalahari has been even harder hit: denied freedom of movement to water and fresh pastures, a staggering 99 per cent of the region's wildebeest and 95 per cent of its hartebeest – at one time second in number only to that of the famed Serengeti plains of East Africa – have disappeared. A compounding tragedy, some believe, is that there is as yet no absolutely conclusive scientific proof that wild game infect domestic stock.

Even less justifiable, it seems, are the newer fences to the north, which will allow cattle into, and confine them within, a limited area to the east of the Okavango River – the last of the region's dry grasslands and home to Africa's largest remaining herds of endangered roan and sable antelope. Cattle farmers here, as elsewhere on the Okavango fringes, have taken to burning the grass of the floodplains to create early greening – a short-sighted and devastatingly destructive habit: apart from heightened competition for food resources, removal of the vegetation allows the Okavango's waters to carry an increased volume of silt to the wetlands' wider reaches, which destroys their aquatic life forms. Further work on these fences has been delayed, however, following an outcry and pending a proper environmental impact study. But whatever the outcome of the latter,

The 'buffalo fence' across the southern reaches of the Okavango Delta just north of Maun has played a vital role in keeping domestic livestock out of the wilderness area, although the original intent was to prevent wild game from venturing south into cattle country.

and however laudable the intent, man-made barriers will continue to go up, which causes deep concern among conservationists: they believe that the decline in wildlife numbers (the deterioration has been dramatic during the past decade) cannot be halted if the animals are hemmed in; many species, they say, need to migrate to water and to more nutritious pastures in the dry months in order to survive. And even so, the chances are the cattle will continue to encroach on the Delta. Livestock is at the very heart of Tswana culture, and the industry, though of far less relative value today than it was before the discovery of diamonds, is a national preoccupation.

The pressure is relentless. Impelled by government policy and foreign loans from donors who believe their money is helping the country's poor, the domestic livestock population (of sheep, goats, donkeys and cattle) has expanded to levels well beyond the carrying capacity of the sandveld, and the rate of desertification is cause for deep concern.

For cattle, it is said, are the earth's most dangerous animals. They're certainly among the most destructive: they need ready supplies and great quantities of water; they are voracious and unselective feeders, stripping the land of its greenery and creating dustbowls in the process; the fences and pesticides they need to keep them free of disease make savage inroads into the wildlife, pollute the water, introduce toxins into the food chain and disrupt the fragile ecological balance. But the steady advance of the ranchlands continues.

According to local conservationist and film-maker Rick Lomba, the number of cattle in the Delta rose from 3 000 to 27 000 over a period of just two years during the early 1990s.

And, as if the wilderness hadn't enough to contend with already, other enemies have done and are doing their worst. Among them:

• The sporting hunter. There is a quota system in force, but apparently the limits in many instances are disregarded, and over-hunting has reached critical levels.

• The poacher – as ubiquitous and lethal

a presence in Botswana as anywhere else in Africa. Poaching for game-meat takes its toll, but generally the off-cut is tolerable. Similarly, ivory hunters (many of whom are from outside the borders), are active, but not so much so that the elephant herds are significantly affected – indeed in some areas they have survived too well, to the detriment of the habitat. Some wildlife species, however, are highly vulnerable; rhino, for example (both the white and the black species) have all but disappeared from the scene despite carefully controlled programmes to reintroduce, nurture and protect them. Poaching is on the increase, though the authorities, with splendid help from the Botswana Defence Force, may yet be able to contain the crisis.

• Deadly pesticides have been used, extensively, for the past four decades, latterly with the blessing of the Food and Agricultural Organization (FAO), to get rid of the tsetse fly. The Botswana government claims that massive animal-spraying is primarily designed to eradicate a *human* health hazard, but the end result is that the northern parts of the Delta can now accommodate domestic livestock, and will inevitably do so in increasing numbers.

• The demands of Botswana's diamond industry (especially the Orapa mine) and the fast-growing town of Maun for water. Highly controversial proposals to siphon off some of the Delta's abundance – notably by dredging the Boro River – have been shelved for the time being, but the mine's underground sources aren't limitless and the worry is that, unless the environmentalists maintain a close and continuous watching brief, the project could be revived at some future date. And, of course, it isn't just the wildlife and the tourist that will suffer: more than 40 000 ordinary people – fisherfolk and cultivators – depend on the swamplands for their very survival.

• The road-building programme. The trans-Kalahari highway will cut through the north-central region, and in particular the wildlife management area adjacent to the Central Kalahari Game Reserve. The boreholes that are due to be drilled along its length will tap precious underground water resources, and

Several local conservation programmes are in place, and most people in the safari community are involved in one way or another.

encourage pastoral settlement that will compete for and eventually degrade the grassland areas.

• Finally tourism, which contributes 40 per cent of formal employment in northern Botswana and US$50 million annually to the national product, but which has been described by one Botswana parks official as 'the greatest threat of all' to the Delta region. The issue, however, is by no means clear-cut: the Delta is certainly becoming an increasingly popular destination, and in the early 1990s plans were being finalized to treble the number of concessionary areas (blocks of land reserved for individual safari firms), which will add substantially to the tourist presence, especially in and around the magical Moremi area. But on balance the scheme could prove surprisingly beneficial: the new 15-year lease arrangement should encourage private operators, long plagued by the need to renew their leases each year, to become more active in long-term conservation programmes. And, of course, tourism generates the income so desperately needed to preserve what are undoubtedly the greatest and most fragile of Africa's wetlands.

OKAVANGO DELTA

Opposite and above: *The water-adapted red
lechwe, found throughout the swamplands.*

The Okavango River is southern Africa's third largest watercourse (after the Zambezi and the Orange), rising in the Angolan uplands to flow south, west and then south again across Namibia's Caprivi 'strip' into Botswana. At the end of its journey it spreads out over the Kalahari sandveld in an immense, fan-shaped inland delta, and the wetlands so created are among the great natural wonders of Africa. Here there are wide, mysterious waterways, tranquil lagoons and palm-graced islands, narrow labyrinthine channels choked by reed and papyrus and by dense mantles of water lilies that bloom gloriously in their season.

The Delta has three fairly distinct regions. In the north-west, around and along the Panhandle – the 'stem' of the fan – are the Okavango's permanent waters, the deep and languidly moving streams, the ox-bow lakes and wooded islands of a pristine wilderness that remains much the same throughout the year. Then there's the lower Delta, whose channels are filled for much of but not all the time, its tree-girded floodplains often covered by grassland that attracts and sustains a great number of buffalo and other herbivores. Finally you have the Delta's outer fringes, sandy ridge-like areas covered by scrub mopane and patches of acacia and blessed by numerous pans. Here, too, the wildlife congregates, especially at the end of the seasonal rains.

At one time in the not too distant past these magical swamplands and their peripheries were home to a stunning variety of animals of both the wetland and dryland kinds. Early travellers reported seeing herds of wildebeest and buffalo tens of thousands strong, elephant and zebra, sable, eland, roan and a host of other antelope together with their attendant predators – lion, leopard, cheetah, hyaena and wild dog.

Today, with the encroachment of man and his cattle ranches, migratory patterns have been disrupted and the numbers are far more modest. But most of the species that the Victorian explorers observed (and hunted) are still represented, integral parts of a fragile ecosystem that remains one of the world's least spoilt and most beautiful wildernesses.

Opposite: Buffalo are among the Delta's most numerous animals, and aggregations of up to a thousand strong are by no means unusual at certain times of the year.

Above: The waterways of the Okavango hide a treasure-chest of unexpected delights, such as this tiny painted reed frog taking refuge in a water lily.

Right: Day-flowering lilies close up for the night as the sun sets over the Boro River near Xaxaba. A different type of water lily, one that opens out by night and has a stronger scent, will soon appear, attracting nocturnal insects through the night hours.

Above: Traditionally, homebuilding is womens' work in Africa. Here a group of them thatch a hut under construction at Jedibe village in the north-eastern Okavango. The home will be built entirely of materials gathered locally.

Right: Basketry is Botswana's premier craft, a tradition handed down from mother to daughter through generations. Sought after as curios by visitors from abroad, the baskets serve as functional items in most Batswana homes.

Right: Silhouetted against a spectacular sky, two anglers try for the last catch of the day.
Below: Mokoro excursions are probably the most rewarding means to explore and enjoy the myriad waterways of the Okavango. They also offer the best chance of seeing the shy and elusive swamp-dwelling sitatunga antelope.

Opposite above and above:
A majestic fish eagle swoops for
supper. These eagles will often capture prey so large they are unable
to take off again, but rather than
relinquish their catch will swim to
shore with the fish firmly gripped
in their talons.

Opposite below: A flight of knob-
billed ducks takes off from the lower
reaches of the Gomoti River near San-
ta-wani, one of the longest established
safari lodges in Botswana.

Right: The saddlebilled stork is one
of the most colourful of the stork
family. It gets its name from the
bright yellow 'saddle' and the base
of its imposing bill.

Opposite: *A cheetah peers out across the floodplain from its hideout at the base of a clump of palms.*

Above: *Although cheetah are usually solitary animals, a female's offspring will remain with her well into maturity as they learn to hunt and fend for themselves. These are the fastest animals on earth, with a reputed top speed of more than 120 km/h, used in short bursts to run down their prey. Should the latter stand its ground, the cat will usually back off.*

Left: *A pair of lionesses doze fitfully in the morning sun.*

Above: Intrepid travellers and their guides make their leisurely way by mokoro up the Boro River into the heart of the Okavango wetlands. Popular with young and old, such do-it-yourself excursions can either be arranged in Maun or from camps such as the curiously (though in some ways aptly) named 'Oddballs'.

Left: A pair of 'plastic mekoro', an environmentally sensitive alternative to the traditional dug-out, at Ker & Downey's Pom Pom camp. Because the manufacture of traditional mekoro results in the destruction of countless huge, old trees each year, both the government and the safari industry are promoting the use of these 20th century immitations.

Opposite above: A relaxing drink at the Fish Eagle Bar, overlooking lily-clad Xaxaba lagoon, ends the day at Gametrackers' Xaxaba camp.

Opposite below: Empty chairs and a cold hearth await the return of the evening game drive at Pom Pom camp. Later, around a blazing log fire, guests will listen to the sounds of the African night and regale each other with safari tales.

Left: *While the lion is generally considered the king of beasts, a leopard sighting remains for many the ultimate wildlife encounter. Few of these spotted cats are seen out in the open like this, at magnificent full stretch: most sightings are limited to a fleeting glimpse of dappled hide or a flicking tail in the dense foliage of a tree.*

Opposite far left, left and right: *Wild dogs are among Africa's most endangered large mammals, their numbers decimated by disease, loss of range and persecution by man. Botswana, however, still has a sizeable population of these most efficient predators, with Mombo camp ranking as perhaps the best place in Africa to see and photograph them. In 1993 there were three different packs in the immediate area.*

Above: Curious and alert, a pride of young lions on Shindi Island watch a herd of lechwe grazing in the distance.
Right: A magnificent kudu bull turns from browsing, seemingly unperturbed by the presence of the photographer. The animal, though, is timid by nature. When disturbed, it utters a sharp bark, raises its tail and makes quickly for cover.

Above: *The sable is one of the most majestic of all the antelope species. Regal and aloof, it occurs widely throughout the northern parts of Botswana, though rarely in any great numbers.*

Left: *The reedbuck is a shy and retiring animal that will often 'freeze' in position in long grass or reedbeds, in the hope that it will go undetected.*

Opposite: Botswana has possibly the largest elephant population in Africa. The country is home to an estimated 50-60 000 of the giant pachyderms.
Above: The pangolin, or scaly anteater, is one of the most unusual creatures of the bushveld. It is also among the rarest sightings: endangered because of tribal superstitions and their use in muti (traditional medicines), the creatures are primarily nocturnal and spend their days sleeping hidden under piles of dead vegetation or in holes in the ground.
Left: A newborn wildebeest calf stands on unsteady legs alongside its mother and other herd members. Although climatic conditions – rain and rising temperatures – can be unpleasant for summertime visitors, they provide bonuses such as lush greenery and the arrival of the young of most species.

Above: *Maun has grown from a dusty little safari centre a few years back, into a modern town with paved roads, shopping malls and multi-storey shopping blocks. It still serves as the headquarters of the country's growing safari business: it is the gateway to* the Okavango wetlands and the adjacent Moremi Game reserve. While the opening of the tarred road through from Nata means the town is now far more accessible to ordinary sedan cars, four-wheel drives still predominate.

Top: While Maun may have leapt into the modern age, one need only drive a few kilometres out of town to find rural Africa and its ancient ways.
Above left: To countless adventurers and safari enthusiasts, Riley's Garage and the next door hotel in central Maun have been an automatic port of call.
Above right: Ostrich farmer George McAllister moves a bundle of day-old chicks. Along with crocodile ranching, the breeding of ostriches is among the fastest-growing of Botswana's less commercial industries.

MOREMI GAME RESERVE

Opposite: *Mopane woodland in autumn.*
Above: *Lioness in quiet mood.*

The limpid waters of the Okavango Delta inundate much of (but by no means all) the Moremi sanctuary, an 1 800 square kilometre expanse of waterway and secluded lagoon, wooded island, floodplain, riverine acacia, dryland mopane forest and open grassland that lies to the north of Maun.

The reserve holds a proud place in the annals of southern African conservation. In the early 1960s the local Tawana people, fully aware of and increasingly worried about the threat posed to their traditional lands by sporting hunters and other intrusive elements, set aside the area as a game sanctuary – one of the few instances in Africa, indeed in the world, of a community voluntarily dispossessing itself of its territorial birthright.

This is big game country. There are no fences around the reserve (though veterinary cordons have made their appearance far to the south), the animals are free to migrate to and from the Chobe park to the north, and at times – especially in the dry months – Moremi plays host to a large proportion of the wider region's 70 000 elephant. Other species abound, among them buffalo and zebra, impala, kudu and tsessebe; reedbuck, waterbuck, lechwe and sitatunga in the wetter parts; the rare roan antelope and the Chobe bushbuck; monkeys and a myriad baboons; lion and leopard, hyaena, wild dog and other predators. The avifauna, too, is quite splendid: around 400 different kinds of birds have been recorded, most prolifically and colourfully on and around the floodplains.

The most prominent of Moremi's several distinctive components is Chief's Island, an enormous (100 by 15-kilometre) game-rich expanse of forest and savanna between the Boro and Santantadibe rivers to the west, in the Delta proper. The island has neither roads nor permanent camps (though a dozen or so operate on and near its fringes), and can best be explored in the company of a professional safari guide.

Visitors can, however, embark on self-drive excursions around the eastern segment of the reserve, along tracks that are sandy and, in the wet season, challenging. Here too, there's a trio of public camping sites and a scatter of inviting private safari lodges.

Right: *A family of giraffes, the tallest mammals on earth, break into their curious rocking-horse gait to gallop swiftly away from the photographer's intrusive helicopter.*
Below: *The Okavango is made up of countless little channels, lagoons, islets and larger islands, but several major waterways spread out fan-like once the Okavango River leaves the Panhandle in the north. Here the Santantadibe River, in the Delta's south-eastern region, flows from a pic-turesque lagoon and downward into the Moremi mopaneveld.*
Below right: *An elephant, glowing golden in the late evening sunlight, makes his way off the Khwai River floodplain into the surrounding woodland.*

Overleaf: A breeding herd of elephants, comprising cows and calves, approaches across the open plains of the Savute marsh, reduced to grassland following the drying-up of the Savute Channel early in the Eighties.

Above: Dust hangs heavy in the air as a buffalo bull noses tentatively forward, issuing challenge to any potential aggressors. Although they appear as docile and content as domestic cattle, these huge creatures are ranked among Africa's most dangerous animals when wounded, cornered or threatened.

Left: Savute is elephant country, and Pump Pan in summer is as good a place as any in the world to observe the behemoths at rest and play. A bull sprays himself with cooling water and others slake their thirsts, while a herd of impala nervously approach in the background.

Right: Close encounters of an elephantine kind are more possible at Savute than elsewhere in Botswana, for here the animals have grown accustomed to vehicles and regularly stroll past almost within arm's reach.

Opposite above: The lions of Savute are almost as renowned as the elephants; prides and even individuals are known by name among the local safari operators. Here a pride pays an early morning visit to the waterhole after a night on the prowl and before finding a shady spot to lie up.

Opposite left: The zebra is the national animal of Botswana, though its numbers have been seriously depleted in recent years through drought, excessive hunting and the veterinary cordon fences that have cut off migratory routes and access to water.

Above: The timid impala is one of the prettiest of the antelopes, though is tends to be disregarded by most gameviewers because it is so commonly encountered. Both browsers and grazers, these versatile animals play an important role in bushveld ecology and adapt well to overgrazed or trampled areas.

Opposite: A large buffalo herd moves along the Chobe River floodplain, preparing to retire into the adjacent woodland during the heat of the day. Towards the end of the dry season, buffalo aggregations numbering as many as a thousand animals are common along the river banks.

Top: Though most of northern Botswana is flat and featureless, several rocky inselbergs in the Savute area break the monotony of the landscape. Here an elephant moves away from the Gubatsaa outcrop after feeding on the rich vegetation along its lower slopes.

Above: A herd of tsessebe take shelter from the midday sun in the shade of a spectacular acacia tree in the heart of Savute.

Left: With the drying of the lower reaches of the Savute Channel in the early Eighties countless animals perished, including many crocodiles and hippos. Today none of these aquatic animals survives in the Savute area, though the upper portion of the Channel, where it flows out from the Linyanti Swamp and holds water throughout the year, remains a haven for them.

Below: A group of bull elephants gathers around the water at a pan in Savute. There is a strict heirarchy in such gatherings, and members of lower status may have a long wait before getting their chance to drink.

Opposite: An impala ram bends to drink while a yellowbilled oxpecker, perched on his shoulder, keeps watch. The relationship is mutually rewarding – the bird is able to feast on ticks and other parasites, which keeps the animals healthy. It also acts as a superb early warning system for its host.

Opposite: A young spotted hyaena keeps watch from near its den, awaiting perhaps the return of clan members from the night's scavenging.

Above: Kudu, impala and helmeted guineafowl quench their thirst at a waterhole in the Chobe National Park, taking comfort in each other's proximity. Most of the wilderness's prey species are particularly vulnerable when drinking, and the nervous tension at such times is almost tangible.

Above right: The yellowbilled kite visits Botswana during the summer months, at which time of the year it is probably the most common of all the country's raptors.

Right: The warthog gets its name from the wart-like protuberances on its face. Females have one pair of warts, males two. The animals are usually found in close-knit family groups; at night they shelter in burrows, which they enter tail first.

Overleaf: Savute's lions are renowned for their hunting abilities, and regularly kill such large prey as adult giraffes, even though the latter are capable of putting up a strenuous defence: their kick can be lethal and several cases are on record of lions being killed in the attempt.

Above: *As the sun sets in the west a lion pride awakens, readying itself for the night ahead. Lions sleep for as many as 20 hours out of 24, and hunt mainly during the hours of darkness.*

Below: *Guests from the Chobe Game Lodge look on while a lone lioness tucks into her kill.*
Bottom: *A warthog sow and her young get down on their knees to enjoy the luxurious new growth after the onset of the summer rains.*

Left: *The sundowner cruise aboard a houseboat, equipped with a fully stocked bar and a selection of hot and cold canapes, offers a romantic ending to the African day. This is one of the most popular excursions offered by most lodges in Chobe.*

Below: *The puku is closely related to the lechwe, but occurs in far smaller numbers and ranks as one of the rarest of the country's antelopes. It is unlikely to be seen anywhere else in Botswana other than along the Chobe River's reaches.*

Opposite: Buffalo are highly gregarious animals and, despite their dangerous reputation, are mild mannered in their relationships with each other. Social harmony is maintained within a dominance heirarchy based primarily on age and seniority.

Left: A redbilled oxpecker probes into the corner of a flinching buffalo's eye. Both redbilled and yellowbilled oxpeckers occur in Botswana.

Below: A pair of curious young lion cubs peer towards the photographer's vehicle. Cubs of this age are particularly vulnerable to predation by rivals such as hyaena, leopard, and even by other lion prides when left alone by their mothers, who must continue to hunt to feed both themselves and their offspring.

Above: *A yellowbilled stork wades through flooded grassland in search of a meal, which it finds by walking with its bill partially open and submerged in the water, stirring the bottom with its foot. It feeds on small fish, larvae and crustaceans.*

Left: *A lesser jacana struts across a lily-covered backwater on the Chobe River. Like the larger African jacana, it too has elongated feet and toes to enable it to walk over the floating lilypads.*

Left: *An immature gabar goshawk stares unblinkingly at a flock of queleas drinking nearby.*

Below: *The African skimmer feeds by flying with its beak opened, the longer lower mandible cutting through the water. When it makes contact with a fish the beak snaps closed, pinioning its victim. Skimmer numbers have dropped alarmingly in recent years, a decline blamed by many on the increasing numbers of powerboats operating in their nesting areas.*

Above: Clouds build up over the Chobe River floodplains at daybreak, promising rain later in the day. Summer storms can be dramatic, with the rolling roar of thunder and brilliant, crashing lightning.
Left: The charming and ubiquitous lilacbreasted roller, familiar to every visitor to Africa.

Opposite: The Chobe is one of the most beautiful of southern African rivers. Downstream it joins the mighty Zambezi for the journey through Zimbabwe and Mozambique to the sea. Upstream it is known as the Linyanti, which forms the border between Botswana and Namibia's Caprivi Region.

MAKGADIKGADI AND NXAI PANS

Opposite: *Giraffe at the Nxai Pan.*
Above: *The bizarre baobab.*

The salt pans of the east-central region are among Botswana's most striking physical features, second only to the Okavango Delta, perhaps, in their visual prominence. Two of them – Ntwetwe and Sowa – are the largest of their kind in the world: great, pancake-flat expanses of sun-blasted terrain fringed by the vegetated 'islands' and 'peninsulas' of an inland sea that, aeons ago, received its waters from the Zambezi, Kwando and Okavango rivers. Now, for most of the year, they are a bone-dry desolation of hard, blindingly white saline sand and mirages that flicker in the tortured air.

But when the summer rains come the salty wilderness undergoes a transformation. Countless waterbirds are drawn to the pools and shallow sheets of water that cover the crusty surface, among them pelicans and enormous flocks of flamingoes. In seasons of poor rainfall the latter are invloved in a life-or-death race against time as their fledglings, too recently hatched, struggle to fly before the last of the water evaporates and the predators move in.

The mineral-rich pans also attract an impressive number of animals. In fact the wider region, despite its inhospitable appearance, supports astonishing numbers of plains game, though the populations are steadily declining as ranchlands encroach on the pasturage and veterinary cordon fences block the migratory routes. The herds congregate on the open grasslands around the Boteti River in the west during the dry months and then, at the start of the wet season, move northwards towards another sequence of pans.

Of these, Nxai is the largest. It too was once part of a lakes complex but is quite different in character from Ntwetwe and Sowa: here, instead of a briny wasteland, there are broad acres of grass and the occasional 'island' of trees, the whole surrounded by forest and savanna woodland.

Nxai's wildlife is similar to that of its southern neighbours, though in most years the complement is enhanced by large (up to 60-strong) groups of giraffe and, at the start of the rains, by the small parties of elephant that filter down from the north.

*Kubu Island (**left**) rises mysteriously and unexpectedly from the featureless salt flats of the Makgadikgadi Pans, a rocky outcrop scattered with grotesque baobab trees (**below**) and ancient stone walls of uncertain origin (**opposite below**). The pans once formed the bed of a vast inland sea, and here it is possible to follow the ancient shoreline and stroll over pebble-washed beaches, that were born aeons ago. At night, when the wind moans through the twisted limbs of the island's baobabs (**below**), it is not difficult to imagine one is listening to the whisperings of the spirits of an ancient, lost civilisation.*

Opposite: *Kalahari lions are reputed to be among the biggest in Africa, and are known for their magnificent black manes.*

Left: *When the rains fall and the Kalahari pans fill, such creatures as this leopard tortoise arrive to take advantage of the all-too-brief season of plenty. Soon waterbirds will flock here from across the continent, drawn by messages carried on the wind.*

Below: *For much of the year Nxai Pan is barren and lifeless, for most of its game has migrated to easier climes. However, once the rainy season begins and its plains grasses grow lush and nutritious, springbok, gemsbok (oryx), zebra and other herbivores congregate here.*

Above: Flamingoes in their tens of thousands arrive to breed in the Makgadikgadi Pans when they flood in years of good summer rainfall. In some years, however, the pans dry out before the chicks are able to fly away. As a consequence the fledglings die in their thousands of starvation and dehydration.

Left: A lone blackwinged stilt picks its way through the shallows of a flooded pan transformed into liquid gold by the setting sun.

Opposite: A jeep track penetrates the seemingly empty wastelands in a remote corner of the Nxai Pan.

Overleaf: Baines' Baobabs are unusual in that these trees rarely grow in such closely grouped clusters. This was once a popular overnight stop for visitors to the area, but camping has not been permitted since the extension of the national park boundaries in 1993.

Above: *Doves and sandgrouse wheel in the sky above a herd of springbok, attracted to a waterhole at one of the Nxai pans. The Department of Wildlife and National Parks has embarked on a programme to instal permanent waterholes throughout the drier regions – Nxai Pan, Makgadikgadi and the Central Kalahari – in an attempt to counter the effects of the veterinary cordon fences, many of which block the wildlife's traditional dry-season routes to water.*

Right: *A black-backed jackal mother and her pups greet each other on her return from a foraging foray.*

Opposite: *A young lion drinks its fill at a pool filled by recent rains. Lions can in fact survive for long periods without water, obtaining all their liquid requirements from the body fluids of their prey. When water is available, though, they will drink copiously.*

Above: *As they stride purposefully across the plains, a pair of giraffes glow golden in the early evening sun. Giraffe markings tend to vary considerably, and their colours darken noticeably with age.*

Right: *Ground squirrels are found only in the drier regions of Botswana, where they survive on a diet of roots, seeds, bulbs and tubers. They use their bushy tails, spread wide and held upright over their backs, as sun shades in the heat of the day.*

KALAHARI

Opposite: *The endearing meerkat.*
Above: *Lion of Deception Valley.*

Most of Botswana is mantled by the sands of the Kalahari Desert, so termed
because, apart from a few perennial springs, the soils are poor, the landscapes
arid-looking: there is no surface water and precious little rain.

It is not, though, a true desert but, rather, an arid savanna wilderness – its broad, largely featureless plains are clad, albeit scantily, by sweet grasses and by patches of
camelthorn, blackthorn and other acacias,.

These great, forbidding places also manage to sustain their wildlife populations, a surprisingly rich diversity of animals – among them springbok and gemsbok, blue wildebeest,
eland, red hartebeest – that are superbly adapted to the bone-dry conditions. Many of
them extract water from such unlikely sources as the dew-covered night-time plants, from
the deep roots of succulents and the moisture-laden wild cucumber and tsamma melon.
Others – carnivores such as lion, leopard, hyaena and wild dog – slake their thirst on the
blood of their prey.

The Kalahari also has its hardy human presence: it is home to the last of the 'traditional'
San (or Bushman) communities, descendants of the once-dominant semi-nomadic hunter-
gatherer inhabitants of the wastelands. The pressures of Western culture, however, have
proved irresistible, and few if any of these people now follow, in any complete sense, the
ways of their ancestors.

Large parts of the Kalahari wilderness – some 75 000 square kilometres in all – have
been set aside as protected areas, which are among the world's wildest and most remote.
The most extensive is the Central Kalahari Game Reserve, along whose southern boundary
lies the smaller and more accessible Khutse sanctuary. The Mabuasehube Game Reserve
and the Gemsbok National Park are much farther to the south. None of these areas has
been well developed for tourism – roads (where they exist) are rudimentary and challenging, facilities are few – yet, for the seeker of solitude and those drawn to the widest of
open spaces, they offer an experience that will linger long in the memory.

Opposite: Though the Kalahari is regarded as a desert because of its low annual rainfall and total absence of surface water, it is in fact well vegetated and, with the recent appearance of permanent man-made waterholes, game populations may in due course swell to their former splendour.
Below: A passing donkey-cart highlights the striking contrast between the traditional mud huts of the village of Letlhakane and the modern road that passes by.

Bottom: Filling the tank at an old, manual fuelpump in the Kalahari village of Rakops.

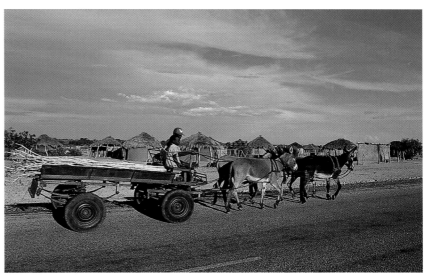

Above: *The Central Kalahari Game Reserve, long closed to all but the resident San people, research scientists and exploration geologists, has in recent years been opened to the public, though visitors must be totally self reliant as there are as yet no tourist facilities. Most tracks, such as this one through Deception Valley, are in good condition, although a four-wheel-drive is essential in places.*

Right: *The puffball flowers of the water acacia, Acacia nebrownii, brighten the Kalahari landscape at the end of the long, dry winter months. The blooms are among the first to announce the arrival of spring.*

Opposite: *Botswana is renowned for its spectacular sunsets, especially during the dry season when dust and smoke from bushfires combine to colour the evening sky.*

Opposite: *Eyes agleam, an alert lioness peers through the fork of a small Kalahari tree.*

Above: *Gemsbok, or oryx, are specially adapted for life in extreme temperatures and can survive without water in desert conditions. They range over huge areas, eating mainly grass but also digging for roots and bulbs and foraging for wild melons, from which they obtain moisture.*

Right: *Although lions are the only social members of the cat family, there is a lot of aggression within groups, in the form of threat displays, vocalisations or even serious fighting.*

Right: *After spending the better part of a day in these lions' company, the photographer crawled on his belly to within two metres of them, eliciting little more than mild curiosity while obtaining this low-level photograph .*

Below left: *Bat-eared foxes use their exceptional hearing to find subterranean prey such as termites and other insects. They also feed on small reptiles and rodents.*

Below right: *A ground squirrel surveys his territory before venturing afield from the safety of his burrow. These animals are preyed upon quite heavily by chanting goshawks and other raptors.*

Opposite below: *Black-backed jackals, persecuted as stock-killers in farming areas, are among the most adaptable of all the carnivores, occuring in all habitat types except forest. They are indiscriminate feeders, eating anything from carrion, small mammals, rodents, reptiles and insects to wild fruits.*

149

Left: *A pair of suricates, left behind to babysit the young while the rest of the family are off hunting, survey their domain from atop the heap of sand excavated from their intricate system of underground burrows.*

Opposite below: *A cluster of ostrich eggs left to incubate in the early morning sun. Often more than one ostrich hen will use the same nest, and the eggs are then incubated and raised by the cock and senior hen.*

Below left: *The Kalahari is a region for the specialist birder – it is home to a confusing array of LBJs (little brown jobs), among them the Sabota lark.*

Below right: *A yellow mongoose ventures forth from its burrow, which is often shared with suricates and ground squirrels.*

Above left: *The red hartebeest is a powerfully built, extremely nomadic antelope able to cover vast distances in search of fresh grazing. It is rarely seen outside of the central and southern Kalahari,*

Left: *This masked weaver has chosen an attractive site to build his nest, into which, when it is completed, he will attempt to entice a female.*

Above: *The green season in the Kalahari is short and sweet, the fresh new foliage attracting browsers such as springbok.*

Left: *The marsh owl is commonly encountered in the grasslands of the vast Central Kalahari, where it preys on such nocturnal rodents as rats and mice.*

Although the Tsodilo Hills are distant and remote, it is worth making the effort of a road journey. A nearby airstrip, with a long walk to the hills (**far right**), offers a viable alternative. A national monument (**right**) and the site of more than 3 500 examples of rock art dating back thousands of years, the paintings are easily accessible and situated in an area still inhabited by Khoisan speaking peoples. Perhaps the most spectacular subject of all is the decorated outcrop known as Van der Post's Panel (below), named after anthropologist Sir Laurens van der Post.

Above: A spectacular sunset sky enhances the featureless landscape embracing the rocky outcrops of Tsodilo Hills. The highest of the hills rises 400 metres above the flat, sandy surrounds.

Left: Stylised paintings of a penguin and whales indicate the ancient artist most probably visited the sea, well over a thousand kilometres to the west of Tsodilo, at least once in his lifetime. Human and animal remains in the shelter indicate that the hills were inhabited as long ago as 19 000 years.

Top: *Rhino are virtually extinct in modern Botswana. These paintings serve as a poignant reminder of a once-prolific species.*

Above centre: *The Tsodilo Hills paintings differ from those of most other areas in their emphasis on animals and geometric motifs, so these dancing people stand out prominently.*

Right: *The 'White Painting Shelter', includes horsemen, possibly a wagon wheel, and an elephant, perhaps depicting a hunt and suggesting the importance of the ivory trade in the area during the 19th Century.*

EASTERN BOTSWANA

Opposite: *A leopard resting after finishing a meal.*
Above: *A lone bull elephant in the Tuli Region.*

Botswana's most heavily populated and economically developed areas lie to the east, along the line of rail leading from Lobatse through a comparatively well watered and fertile land to the Zimbabwean border in the north.

This is where you'll find most of the urban centres, biggest and arguably most attractive of which is Gaborone, one of the smaller but fastest growing of the southern hemisphere's capital cities. When Botswana celebrated its independence some three decades ago Gaborone was little more than an over-grown village of some 6 000 souls, though for years it had functioned as the administrative headquarters of one of the country's two provincial divisions. It's now a handsome and flourishing little metropolis that has been ranked, by a prestigious international business magazine, among the world's 'cities of the future' – a trim, modern place of modestly elegant buildings and tree-lined thoroughfares, beautifully laid out to cope with the expansionary demands of the new millennium.

Farther up the line are the lesser towns: Mahalapye, Palapye, Selebi-Phikwe and Francistown, the country's second biggest and most industrialized centre, owing its prominence to its strategic position astride the main north-south land route. The complex of eastern towns also encompasses several 'traditional villages' that are, in fact, substantial settlements that have served (and still serve) as the capitals of the various Batswana tribal groupings. Serowe, with its circular, attractively thatched, courtyard-enclosed vernacular houses and a population of 50 000, is the largest, perhaps most picturesque, and notable as the birthplace of Sir Seretse Khama, Botswana's first president.

To the east of the railway line, between the Shashe and Limpopo rivers, is a wedge-shaped chunk of ruggedly beautiful countryside known as the Tuli Block. The rangeland is fairly heavily populated and intensively farmed, but there's still room for two or three of southern Africa's larger and more inviting private game reserves. Prominent among these are luxurious Tuli Safari Lodge and Mashatu Game Reserve, equally sophisticated and famed for its elephant herds.

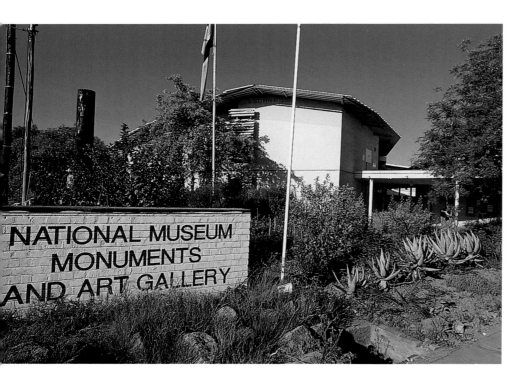

Left and below left: *The National Museum and Art gallery in the capital city of Gaborone houses impressive displays depicting the country's early history, its wildlife, and traditional and modern art forms.*

Top and right: *The Gaborone mall in the heart of the rapidly spreading city is a bustling centre fringed by modern shops, restaurants and a prominent hotel, though hawkers and vendors – offering anything from both locally made and imported African curios, handmade jewellery and leather sandals – certainly add to the vibrant buzz of the place.*

Only a short detour off the main road north from Gaborone is the village of Odi, where a community project producing woven mohair rugs and wall-hangings has grown into a thriving cottage industry. Visitors are welcomed to the sprawling workshops, and can watch every step of the process, from the washing, dying and spinning of raw wool to the weaving of both simple and complex designs. On sale in the showrooms alongside is a large selection of spectacular designs depicting African tribal life.

Left: *Vendors and hawkers display their colourful wares at an informal street market in Francistown.*
Below: *Although heavily industrialised Francistown has little to offer in the way of tourist attractions, it is a popular stopover for travellers on the road to Maun and the game parks farther north. The Thapama Lodge on the outskirts of the city offers comfort and sophistication.*

Above: *Apart from the Okavango and Chobe/Linyanti complexes in the north, there are no perennial rivers in Botswana. The spasmodically flowing Shashe, seen here, is typical of the majority.*

Right: *When heavy rains do fall, Botswana has to make the most of them and storage facilities, such as the Shashe Dam near Francistown, have been constructed throughout the eastern part of the country to capture the runoff.*

Above: A road maintenance crew, dragging a tree in an attempt to 'grade' the rutted gravel track, goes about its work in the eastern Tuli Block.

Left: To the Botswana nation, the Khama family gravesite atop Thathaganyane hill in the centre of Serowe village is a sacred place. The climb to the top affords spectacular views of the surrounding countryside and over the traditionally laid-out village below. It is forbidden to photograph the graves without prior permission.

Above: The Khama III Memorial Museum in Serowe contains memorabilia of the Khama royal family as well as displays of Ngwato and San culture.

Left: The privately-funded Khama Rhino Sanctuary, about 20 kilometres outside Serowe, has been established as a refuge for the country's few remaining rhinoceroses. Currently home to a small breeding group of the white variety, the trustees hope eventually to obtain black rhinos too, with the ultimate aim of re-establishing both types in the wild.

Opposite: *Eland are Africa's largest antelope – males weigh up to 750 kilograms – but despite their size and apparent ungainliness they are extremely agile. They are also excellent jumpers, able to clear a two-metre fence with ease.*

Above: *The eastern part of Botswana differs markedly in topography from the rest of the country. Rugged, rocky hills and spectacular scenery are a hallmark of the Mashatu Game Reserve and Tuli Lodge area, in the northern Tuli Block bordering on South Africa and Zimbabwe.*

Right: *The diminutive klipspringer is a specialist rock dweller, its hooves specially adapted to a life of leaping from rock to rock. Common in the Tuli Block, it is unlikely to be seen anywhere else in Botswana because of a lack of suitable habitats.*

Above and left: *Set under sprawling nyalaberry, or mashatu, trees, Tuli Lodge offers simple but comfortable accommodation amid craggy rock outcrops near the banks of the Limpopo River. The lodge is known for its spectacular gardens, which proved so tempting to visiting game - particularly elephants – that electrified fencing was installed. The focal point of the camp is the Tree Bar, built around a huge mashatu tree.*

Below and bottom: *Mashatu, the largest privately owned game reserve in southern Africa is part of the Mala Mala/Rattray Reserves stable, offers both a traditional tented safari accommodation (**below**) and luxury airconditioned bungalows and suites (**bottom** left) sited in different parts of the reserve; both offer the ultimate in comfort, service and cuisine; meals are taken either in thatched dining-rooms overlooking floodlit waterholes (**bottom right**), or alfresco in the palm-fringed enclosures, or bomas.*

Left: *Eland are gregarious animals, encountered in herds up to 100 strong, though they are more usually seen in groups of five to 20.*

Opposite below: *Mashatu Game Reserve is home to the largest privately conserved population of elephants in the world, though at certain times of the year these range quite widely across the international boundary into parts of Zimbabwe. The population, estimated at 700 to 900 animals, gather in large herds – aggregations of several hundred are often seen.*

Below: *Striking rock formations set the Mashatu Game Reserve scenically apart from most of Botswana's other wildlife areas.*

Overleaf: *Elephants quench their nighttime thirst and spray cooling mud over themselves at a waterhole in the Mashatu reserve.*

173

Alphabetical arrangement is word-by-word. Page references in *italic* refer to photographs.